The
Secret Parent

The hidden truths of life, parenting and childhood through the eyes of a Kids Life Coach

---

ZELNA LAUWRENS

First published in the United Kingdom
in 2018 by Life Studio for Kids Publishing

Further books by this author include:

Zeal the Zebra Shows His True Colours

The Zeal Challenge for Teens

The Equal Zeal System for Parents

A CIP Catalogue record for this book is available from the British Library.

ISBN: 978-1-9164630-0-4

Life Studio for Kids Publishing

www.kidslifestudio.com

DEDICATION

This book is dedicated to my nephew Ayden
and nieces Tayah, Lucy, Darcey, Holly & Caitlyn.

The day God decided I was to be the Mother of Many,
he didn't stop there.

He also blessed me with you to keep my heart full.

♥

CONTENTS

ACKNOWLEDGMENTS

If you have contributed to The Secret Parent, in any way, know that you are in my heart and mind. I may not mention your name here, but your actions are forged in my memory and I value your love. You know who you are.

To my husband Stephen, you have patiently held me with unconditional love and breathing space until I was ready to share the hidden truths that you have always known. This is just one of the many reasons I love you.

To my parents. The day I was born, you set my path on a trajectory that encouraged me to always be the leader of my own life. Thank you for your love and giving me the strength to follow through on my dreams.

To my fuzzy cuzzy Bradley. Born two weeks apart, your belief in me is a reflection of just how much I believe in you. Thank you for always walking by my side with no expectations and just letting me be me.

To my good friends Abigail, Sheridan & Saritha. Thank you for sharing your time so willingly to cast your eyes on my work before the rest of the world. It means so much to me knowing that you helped me shape the contents of this book with your valuable input.

To my mentor Iain, your wisdom and encouragement as you diligently spent time with me working through my chapters, allowed me to speak my truth with my long-term business goal in sight.

To my special friends Taryn, Robyn and Kent, your coaching, support and encouragement kept my momentum going when some days it felt easier to give up. Thanks for holding the space for me so intentionally, while you allowed me to figure things out for myself with a gentle nudge here and there.

To my global Team Zealers. I trained you to be Kids Life Coaches but without you taking action, there would be no impact. I feel so humbled knowing that you are standing by my side as "Secret Parents" changing the world one child at a time. I am so proud of you all!

To God. Once I didn't believe but now I do. I realise that the road I have walked is the one less travelled but it was never really lonely because You have always been beside me every step of the way.

There is a lovely
African proverb
that says:

*'It takes a village
to raise a child.'*

PREFACE

How many people does it take to raise a child?

African culture recognises that parenting is a shared responsibility - a communal affair - not just the concern of parents or grandparents, but of the extended 'family'.

Being a South African, this proverb resonates with me. Now living in the UK, I run an organization which impacts children globally and I have made it my shared responsibility to raise awareness of the role each of us plays in nurturing children to be the best version of themselves.

In light of this, I want to start by explaining to you what my book doesn't cover. It doesn't cover tips for building children's self-esteem. It doesn't cover parenting tips. It doesn't cover how to discipline children or how to get them to listen. It doesn't cover how to get children to be more mindful or less stressed. It doesn't cover impractical research that looks good on paper, but often contradicts good old fashioned common sense.

What is does cover is my personal story. One that gives a snapshot of my view on life, parenting and childhood. It shares my own "secrets whispered out loud" which have in the past held me back from finding and living my purpose fully. I share the deepest parts of myself like my struggle with mental illness and how not being a biological mother changed my life trajectory.

This book puts childhood into perspective through the real-life stories of the inspirational children I have had the privilege of learning from as a Kids Life Coach. These have included street

1

children, indulged children of foreign diplomats, the mentally & physically challenged, victims of child trafficking, bipolar teens and sociopathic preschoolers.

All of them have one thing in common. They too have a story to tell and it was only when they whispered it out loud to me as their Life Coach, that their own inner truth set them free. They rebranded their childhood, by learning how to make better choices relating to the parts of their lives they had control over. They learnt that your true worth is not derived from who you are but more importantly from who you choose to be.

I empowered each of these children with a practical recipe to use anywhere, anytime to rebrand the parts of their childhood that were holding them back. The real-life stories and examples I share in this book are related to topical childhood challenges and are interwoven with the practical methods that are based on my coaching recipe for children that can be easily applied.

Each chapter will share my personal experiences and I will relate it to a hidden truth that people often don't speak about, so that you can gain practical insight into the realities of being a child and what you can do about it. This book is about giving adults the tools to coach children to build their own positive childhood but first you need to understand why this is necessary.

Babies are born with their destiny to be inspired contributors to our world already in place

Just for a moment, imagine a world where children grow up into the adults they deserve to be. Where they understand their potential and know their value so that they can become inspired contributors to mankind. Where any secret, big or small is used as their fuel for future success rather than holding them back.

How many children right now who are fully able, talented and whole, might be making plans to take their own life as you are reading this sentence? All because they feel unworthy, unloved, neglected or 'different'. All because they have a secret that they cannot tell because they simply don't believe anybody will listen. They fear being judged. Or worse yet, that if they do tell, their life will be destroyed.

The fact is that family life as we know it is disappearing all over the world. Technology is sapping away quality time spent together. The media is exposing children to the truths of the dark scary world of terrorism, murder and natural disasters. Stress, anxiety and depression are no longer a club exclusively for adults. They are having an impact on our children with suicide rates soaring, self-harm becoming the norm, eating disorders and addictions stealing their precious moments and preventing them from becoming adults living a life of fulfilment.

All of this can actively be linked back to stress, which has become a silent killer that is linked to the six chronic causes of death: *heart disease, cancer, lung ailments, accidents and liver cirrhosis,* with the sixth and scariest one being suicide.

Suicide has now become a global phenomenon in all regions of the world and is not limited to age, race, gender or culture. Something has to be done and it starts with each of us whispering our secrets out loud.

A foundation for a healthy adult life starts in childhood

Why wait until a child needs to be medicated for depression or a mental illness or they need therapy for being bullied or they need remedial lessons for falling behind in class?

Most issues in childhood can be prevented simply by giving children a practical and tangible toolkit that empowers them to take control of their life. By energising children's ambitions from a young age, they will have all it takes to rise to the level of their dreams even when life may knock them down.

The truth is that life can be hard and as adults we don't always have the power to change the obstacles that children may face. What we do have though, is the ability to equip them by educating, motivating and inspiring them to rise above life's challenges and turn them into a learning experience that builds their resilience.

There are so many children who are living lives full of potential, despite the circumstances that threaten to weigh them down. These children are living their dreams and inspiring others to do the same. There are also adults who are leading successful lives despite miserable childhoods.

What is it that sets them apart and makes them able to be the leader of their own life by contributing to humanity even when life has been hard for them? The answer is simple. They have made the choice to give the best parts of themselves to the world and to not live entrapped in a victim mentality.

Most people when asked what the opposite of happiness is might respond with "depression, gloom, sadness, misery, unhappiness or sorrow". In my opinion, when you are not happy, you are empty. You lack direction and purpose. You feel like a boat adrift at sea without a rudder. You move through your days devoid of emotions that inspire you. You are simply living to tick the boxes just to start the day all over again tomorrow.

When you find your own purpose you need to shine your light to give others permission to do the same

So often adults make bad decisions based on belief systems created in their childhood and they form opinions, incorrect assumptions and skewed perceptions because they are unaware of any other way.

Whether living homeless on the streets or in a palatial mansion, happiness can be found. Adults think that they know the recipe yet how many are walking around as zombies, empty and lacking in purpose? They have all the trappings of wealth but they are slaves to the machine and they have forgotten their inherent need to love and live life with happiness.

These adults who become parents, do their utmost best to cultivate happiness in their children and sometimes this reflects as a power imbalance of toys, possessions and expensive holidays or experiences and the best schools but very little quality time spent together.

For instance, if we look at adult mental health, it is estimated that 50% of adults were diagnosed with mental health problems in childhood. I believe that the problems that are currently overflowing into adulthood can be prevented and that adults could benefit from being educated in the skills for not only picking up when a child is at risk, but also to prevent things before they start going drastically wrong.

Why wait until children look back on their childhood, and wish some things had been different? Different parents? A better education? More support? Better health? Better friends? Better choices? Why let them blame their childhood experiences for their repetitive patterns of destructive behaviour when they become adults? Why let them turn into grown-ups who abandon their dreams and settle for mediocre because life dealt them a set of cards they didn't know how to play?

There are so many unhappy adults wasting their lives away because they simply know no other way. I also can't help but notice how many so called "leaders in power" are making poor decisions based on faulty childhood beliefs that no longer serve them.

Besides that, there is a distinct lack of role models and this is leading children to lose the true essence of their identity. When we look at the media we see many examples of so called "stars" who are stealing our children's minds with their inappropriate behaviour and lack of morals and values.

Children need tour guides in life
to show them all the best attractions
without having to waste time figuring it out

As a Kids Life Coach, the children that I have spent time with over the last two decades, have shown me glimpses of happiness and I have also seen great emptiness. I have seen tears and massive smiles. I have seen so much potential that is often hidden from the world because of lack of opportunity.

If we want to create a world that thrives and not just survives, it starts with coaching children to adapt to circumstances and make choices that are based on a healthy foundation of a solid self-esteem.

Perhaps this can in future be seen as our long-term antidote to overflowing prisons, terrorism and abuse of power in leaders.

So, a very relevant question would be, how do we coach a child to choose the path of inner peace and happiness when their outer world is in turmoil and they are up against things they simply cannot control?

For example, the children who are forced to be child soldiers in the Central African Republic or those as young as 7 working in cobalt mines in the Congo for stretches of up to 12 hours. Or the ones who are abused, abandoned, bullied, neglected, traumatised. They all have reasons to be unhappy, yet I believe they still have one choice nobody can take away from them - that is the power to choose the thoughts that are the building blocks to their future.

This path is never easy for damaged, hurt and broken children, but they can be coached to take control of the one thing that nobody else has the right to control for them, and that is their mind.

Coaching children is not about discounting the severity of any challenge that they are facing. It is about putting things into perspective for them and opening them up to future possibilities based on hope.

You are already speak the language of childhood because you were a child once

I have a question for you....

Did you know that you are already an expert in childhood? No matter what child you are in contact with, you can get the positive results that I am speaking about.

"How?", you may ask? I want to reassure you, that you don't need to be a parent or have a psychology degree, because *you* were a child once and this perfectly positions you to tap into your own inner child. I believe that every single adult has the power within them to be a "Secret Parent" by using their own personal experiences to inspire children to overcome their obstacles. It does however take commitment to first clearing your own misplaced perceptions about life before you can help children clear theirs.

Rest assured, there is no need to walk around as an adult professing to be the walking, talking billboard for responsibility and making good choices all of the time. If you have built your own life around being perfect, you are setting the children who are in your sphere of influence up for failure.

Just like any great brand, you will make mistakes. Take Richard Branson's failed business venture, Virgin Cola, that declared a soft drink war on Coke. He said, "I consider our cola venture to be one of the biggest mistakes we ever made - but I still wouldn't change a thing." We don't remember him for his failure, but we remember him for his subsequent successes and the fact that he learnt from his mistake and moved along.

Life is about making mistakes, failing miserably, heartache and sadness. I have had my fair share of all of these. Sugar coating this for children will only set them up for disappointment when life does eventually knock them down. Life is made all the richer when we learn from experience and it is often the hardest lessons that give us our biggest personal growth.

The truth is that wrapping children in cotton wool by protecting them from the hard knocks of life is counterproductive. Not only is this disempowering, but it doesn't help to build their immunity to future hardships which are inevitable in life and help to build their resilience.

I have learnt that rebranding childhood is about channeling your own negative or positive story to recreate a child's story. We all have positive and negative stories from our own personal experiences as children and we need to use those to help children to have the best childhood they can. This is about taking the best parts of yourself and celebrating them with absolute reckless abandon.

Why is it that adults are still so scared of failing and why is it that we judge each other so heavily? All of us actually have one thing in common and that is to find happiness, yet we shy away from asking for help when we need it because we are scared of appearing weak.

Just like children who are over exposed to adversity, those that are sheltered miss out on the opportunity to learn. We need to be telling them the truth behind the ugly truth and then some more truth. This is the only way to equip them to stand upright even when their world is having an earthquake, to open their eyes to the realities of life. Once they are aware, they will be better prepared with a road map for making better choices based on what is already familiar.

Sugar Coating life for children does more damage than good

As adults, we need to help children to ignite the fire inside them so that they can find their path to success by building their own personal brand from a young age. Think of any great brand that has become a household name - McDonald's, Disney, Nike.

How did they become famous? They had a strategy. Success in life is much the same. It is about managing our future aspirations, and the only way to do this is to think, act and plan like a leader from the outset.

The earlier we can get children thinking about who they are and what they want to be known for, the quicker they will succeed. Although success can be defined in broad brush strokes, ultimately it means to wake up each day feeling inspired to live life to the fullest.

This can be perfectly true for both the billionaire with multiple companies lavishing in his yacht on the Med or the penniless surfer having the beach as his front yard and living a stress free life. Both are a success by their own definition so long as they are happy.

Coaching children is about helping them to define themselves based on what they want and not other peoples' expectations or demands. This starts with you as an adult, becoming the leader of your own life first based on creating a checklist of your core strengths and maximising them.

Don't make your bad choices, disappointments or regrets the catalyst for forcing children to walk a path that you had always wished for, but that may not be suitable for them.

So many young university students feel coerced into studying for a degree that they didn't want to pursue in the first place. They were not given the luxury of making choices based on their hearts desire and this is often the deep seated cause of their eventual burn out, resulting in them changing careers anyway.

Rebranding your childhood is about taking the good and bad parts to shape the best version of yourself

Building our life is not a one off thing. It is a lifelong process based on putting a solid foundation in place in childhood. This is made up of spending time working out how to define yourself without compromising your core values.

Rather than letting children blend into their discouraging mass of peers making bad choices just to be accepted, they need to create their own unique advantage for getting attention by coming up with their own value proposition for their life. This is especially true for those children who have been negatively labelled and they will have to keep reinforcing their values and skills by taking up new roles and assignments that will give them more positive exposure overtime and change the faulty perception others have of them.

I am on a mission to change the way we look at childhood. Rather than focus on what can go wrong, what has gone wrong or what is going wrong, and trying to fix it, we need to be giving children a toolkit to build their own life of purpose. We were all put on this earth to leave a legacy by serving humanity and it doesn't matter how young or how old, it starts with taking responsibility for our own life first.

When you walk your own walk and talk your own talk in truth and integrity, children will follow

I have hope for every child because no matter their background, circumstances or abilities, they can create a legacy of their own. No matter how big or small their dreams are, with hope driving their desire they can step into their power.

Hope is our secret weapon against war, hunger, strife, heartache and fear. Hope cures the broken and comforts the poor. By reading this book, you may become that one very important person to give a child hope. You have the choice to become "The Secret Parent" alongside me. You never know the extent and influence of your reach because I believe hope can be found where you least expect to find it.

I am trusting that this book will motivate you to be a world-changer by supporting children to become leaders. You can start simply by living your own life with purpose. Take the time to rebrand your own childhood by questioning your own belief systems if you need to, so that you can show children how to actively do the same.

Children need you to be the shining beacon of light that guides them to accountability for their own happiness by actively being a participant in life yourself. Find your own inner peace and use that inner calm to be a good role model. With so much chaos in our world, children are looking for a safe harbour and this is you.

Changing our world doesn't mean we all have to be doing big things. Changing our world means us all doing small things consistently.

Changing our world starts with one child at a time because that child could be our next:

Mother Theresa, Martin Luther King, Ghandi, Nelson Mandela, Winston Churchill, William Shakespeare, Florence Nightingale, Albert Einstein, Elvis Presley or Oprah Winfrey.

We don't yet know the extent and reach of our influence, so every child no matter their circumstances deserves to be uplifted in the same way. They need mentorship, guidance, unconditional love and acceptance to become the leaders of their own life. They need you! So thank you for investing your time in reading this book and being the change in our world that we need!

1

Mother of many

Hidden Truth:
Parents can be selfish without realising

I remember that life-changing moment, that split second that determined the path my life was to take because I lost hope. Looking back now, at the age of 26, I didn't understand in that moment, looking into the eyes of the man I loved, that I would one day be okay with not having children of my own.

"We will never have children." These were the words that echoed over and over in my mind as my husband's face looked up at me, his blue eyes framed by our newly renovated kitchen. I was standing a few feet taller than him, on a step leading into our lounge. My backdrop framed by plush white sofa's. The kind that didn't welcome children's sticky fingers and were perfectly imperfect for a home that hadn't yet seen their casual interference.

Animated floral curtains that matched my personality of being outspoken, adorned our windows, but at that moment my world crumbled and for once I was speechless. I felt the pain and grief tearing at my husband's heart. I saw the truth in his eyes. That hard hitting truth that we were both too scared to whisper out loud. That hope was all we had and that hope wasn't a strategy.

Being married for almost two years, we had done what every newly married couple is expected to do. We had tried to fall pregnant, but unlike our friends, nothing had happened. After a battery of tests and visiting the top fertility specialist in South Africa, we had discovered that our options were slim. IVF, IVF or IVF or more commonly known as Invitro Fertilization.

The stress was immense and the financial, emotional, mental and social pressure was tantamount to slow torture. As soul mates and best friends, my husband and I decided to "pass" on the invitation to flood my body with hormones and to attempt to harvest sperm to create life. If it was God's will, then we would fall pregnant naturally.

Of course, God had his own plans and as I write this, you are witness to how being the mother of none eventually led me to indirectly be the mother of many. Everything in life can shape us or break us and not having children in the traditional sense did both to me. Only now do I see the immense strength that I have because of it.

Since we assumed that conception wasn't about to happen anytime soon without the intervention of science, this was our catalyst for making the decision to pack up our suburban home in Johannesburg and run away to London. My husband was fortunate enough to have ancestral rights through his grandfather and so getting a visa was purely a formality.

With both of us in solid careers, the owners of multiple properties, driving good cars and with a newly renovated home brimming with carefully chosen furniture, we did what few people would do. We rebelled in the only way we knew how.

Sometimes circumstances hijack our original plans to show us new opportunities

We decided to nurse our secret of infertility by running away to a foreign country where questions could easily be avoided and conversations relating to why we weren't yet "breeding" could be limited to nil. Little did I know that this place would become our haven and also the birth place of my global Kids Life Coaching business.

We told nobody. The precious truth was ours to share as husband and wife as we packed up our perfect life into storage and made the decision to leave our two beautiful dogs with my parents in Durban. Until then our dogs were the closest we ever came to being parents. Over the years we were blessed with many more dogs to enter our hearts, but these two remain top of mind as our first born "kids" as we enjoyed them when our marriage was still relatively free from the stress of trying to conceive.

These two delightful pets were our practice run in parenting and so leaving them behind was not a decision we took lightly. Yet, it was something we needed to do, to save ourselves from the torment of staying in a newly created story with a very uncertain ending.

Our extended "adventure" to England, which culminated in me moving from school to school as a supply teacher, was a very convenient and welcome buffer. It saved us having to reveal the real truth behind why we would give up our jobs we loved and exit our comfort zone so hastily.

We were fortunate to have a very fatherly fertility specialist, who encouraged us to do this travelling for a couple of years, and to worry about "manufacturing" our children on our return. He was a proud father in his mid-fifties with greying hair to prove it and his son played rugby for a leading national team that rivalled our favourite team the Natal Sharks.

He was tonic for our soul and he made our short trip through the medicated passages of the fertility clinic on a weekly basis more bearable. His jokes and light hearted banter that made us feel instantly at ease even in the most invasive of scenarios were a rare quality in a gynaecologist. The huge financial investment now seems worth it just to have met him. A kind soul who manufactures babies for the childless. A selfless act that is peppered with purpose.

Being responsible sometimes means doing what is irresponsible

Whilst we were excited at the fun prospects of being "travellers", devoid of formal responsibility for a while, we knew that this would only be a temporary Band Aid that eased our pain. Still, there was a calm inner glimmer of hope that when we returned to reality after our two year sabbatical from everybody's probing questions, the fertility treatments and IVF might work.

In the two years that followed in England, we had wild crazy times and we were care-free and very much admired by our friends we had left behind in South Africa. The ones who were changing dirty diapers, warming up bottles and doing night feeds. We had traded all of this for backpacks, late drunken nights, long road trips, camping in the rain, fine dining and short breaks to Europe. Our life was an adventure with endless freedom or so it seemed to the people who only saw what we wanted them to see.

The world of parenting has many doors to step through and it can become overwhelming

So when we returned, we thought everything would be okay. We believed that having a baby would be as simple as forking out our hard earned cash for the treatments we needed. It didn't prove as easy as that, because after considering the risks and speaking to support groups where couples were nursing their wounds of the loss of what could have been, we saw the real truth.

The chances for us were slim and the stories of disappointment from the couples we spoke to cemented our decision to choose each other as husband and wife instead. We heard stories of heart breaking pain, as many ladies fell victim to their menstrual cycle after a lengthy process of implanting a fertilized embryo in their womb.

It wasn't something I wanted and I don't regret making the decision. Celebrating the birth of a child conceived in a petri dish just seemed vaguely unsuitable for my black and white personality.

For the husbands, the process was humiliating and the very intimate love making act that is supposed to unite husband and wife was bastardized by the sterility of fertilizing eggs and sperm in a laboratory that defied masculinity.

We didn't want to be part of what we perceived as the marital discord, the medical side effects and the economic pressure associated with this process. It was a decision we didn't take lightly, but it was no doubt what saved our marriage from the strain of disappointment month after month (Around 30% of women below the age of 35 falling pregnant this way and this decreasing to a mere 1 - 13% chance for women over 40).

Your adversities are your biggest gift because they are moulding you for a greater purpose.

Although I also remember short spurts of highs and lows in my early twenties, the second time I sank into an intense depression I was in my thirties. We had returned from our sabbatical in England two years prior. We were financially secure, I was well groomed, living in a palatial home, driving a luxury German Sedan, teaching half day and running my dream business coaching children. I had no idea that my "childlessness" would knock me down when I expected it the least.

I had been fine, but I started feeling like a puppy who had peed on the carpet and had her nose rubbed in it. In my world it seemed like everybody with a vagina was popping babies, and I gained a heightened sense of frustration and generalized irritation.

I used to frequently utter the statement: "She doesn't deserve to have kids. I would be a way better mother!" I became bitter and intolerant of parents who were doing a "bad" job, messing up their children's lives and even more so, I started questioning why school girls, drug addicts and HIV infected women were falling pregnant when I wasn't able to.

Life had dealt me a card I no longer wanted to play. I wanted so desperately to go with the status quo, which had conditioned me to believe that you date, get engaged, get married and have babies. No amount of praying, bargaining and filling my life with whatever remedy or treatment I could find, was doing the trick and my punishment for trying so hard was a sense of failure.

I was a perfectionist and bluntly stated, a control freak. My inability to control the fact that my husband and I could conceive naturally was like having root canal treatment without anaesthetic. It was then that the first signs of bitterness reared their ugly head and I started delving into far too much alcohol consumption on weekends and on the opposite extreme far too little sleep.

I was renowned for lining 10 tequilas on the bar counter and downing them in one go. For some this could be termed stupid. For me I now see it as a shroud that masked the real truth. I simply didn't want to feel the pain. I wanted to dampen the confusion I felt in my mind and so drinking large amounts of alcohol in a social setting became my crutch.

I term myself a social alcoholic and no longer partake in this pastime. Many reflect on this as strange, but it is a decision that has cleared my mind and allowed me to actually reflect on life as the truth that it is.

Needless to say, after a while, I started resenting our decision to choose to not partake in IVF and so I prompted our visit to two more top fertility specialists in South Africa for second and third opinions. Unfortunately, their bedside manner was not as conducive to taming our anxiety as our previous grey haired doctor had been, and so our dignity along with our hope was shattered.

The chances were still slim, so our decision remained intact to choose childlessness over and above polluting my body with chemicals that had no guarantee of giving us the results we wanted.

The truth always has a way of unravelling itself

The truth we had hidden for so long started unravelling at the seams as people questioned why we didn't have children. We shared our struggles with those who lent a genuine ear and most of the time, our answers were met with a shake of the head in pity or unhelpful suggestions to adopt or foster. The consistent response was that people actually didn't know how to react and it made them more uncomfortable than it made us.

Well-meaning parents with children of their own would tell us not to give up. They would encourage us to try IVF. They would remind us that if we didn't try, we could be missing out on the best thing in life. To be blunt - they only ignited my resentment towards parents and I started seeing them as an exclusive club and my husband and I were the non-members, with limited benefits.

Like the time good friends of ours hosted a birthday party for their son. We had always been involved in his life and had often baby sat since he was 8 months old, so celebrating his party with him was a definite consideration for us and something we had always done. Then one year, when we weren't invited and we asked why, the answer did little to appease my unsettling judgement that parents can be unknowingly selfish. "You aren't parents" my friend said. End of story. No more discussion.

It was almost as if this friend of ours, who is no longer a friend, didn't understand that we needed to feed our love in and through other people's children. Yet this concept was entirely foreign, as to her and the other parents it must have seemed unusual for a "childless" couple to want to be at a kiddies' birthday party without children of their own. It was evident that she had humoured us previously, but when we eventually didn't fall pregnant, she took a stand to separate us from the clan of parenthood.

This was the first time I can remember being discriminated against unfairly but it wasn't the last. Much of the exclusion we found was much closer to home and came from the places we would have least expected. Sadly, it is all too common that parents nest down with their own little families and they lose all concept of space and time. The truth is that in building their own family, they break down bridges forged over years that can never be fully repaired.

Substituting one thing for another isn't always the solution

I don't know where my sense of fortitude came from, but it was just as I was due to turn 30, that I started realizing that if I was to live my purpose, I had to let go. I was a stubborn one though and of course this was not an easy notion for me, habitually trying to take control of every situation.

Having children was one area that I wasn't able to control, so I channeled my maternal energy into getting my body into shape with a personal trainer and into birthing my first business coaching children.

Both of these pursuits would steal my attention and distract my nagging need to be a mother. They appeased me, if only for a while, but they were a welcome distraction from the endless yearning in my heart.

The plus side was that my need for perfection translated into me quickly and easily building up a good reputation as a passionate Kids Life Coach and the referrals were flying in faster than a jet takes off on a runway. I was inundated with interest and soon I quit my much loved teaching career, moving into my business full time as the first Kids Life Coach in South Africa.

At the height of my career, I was coaching 15 individual children during the week and 45 in groups on the weekends. I was loving it, and working with other people's children allowed me to get rid of my frustrations through a healthy outlet. I was making a difference and I was naturally talented at it. I suppose I equated it to parenting in a way but without the strings attached. It felt rewarding and I was fulfilled. I also had the money to prove it and I liked what it gave me - the recognition, the freedom, the respect. But what it didn't give me was peace of mind.

I soon garnered the interest of the media because of my glowing testimonials and I appeared on a multitude of TV & Radio programs as well as being cited in major newspapers and magazines as an expert in the field of coaching children. Since this was an unknown field and with me being the first Kids Life Coach in South Africa, this catapulted me to the status of "mini-stardom" that gifted me with respect in the localized child well-being industry.

My voice of passion and purpose as a spokesperson for children was being heard and I was enjoying every minute. I loved the limelight, and meeting TV presenters and Radio DJ's and other interesting people was a calling card for my inflated ego.

With my new-found popularity came boundless energy that drove me forward to success. I became distracted from wanting to fall pregnant and started repeating the affirmation: "My business is my baby." I reasoned with myself that I too was experiencing the sleepless nights that new parents had. I was also changing "diapers" as I dealt with the "smellier" side of business – the accounts and administration.

True abundance is never about money.
It is about quality of life.

I flung myself so far into my work that it became an obsession for me, with long hours to prove it. All the while, I was earning money in abundance and with confidence as my trump card I made the decision to make the next step.

After working with a business coach, I took the plunge into "franchising" my Kids Life Coaching concept. A cautionary tale is that even my coach didn't "buy" into my vision to change the world. She insisted I think smaller to avoid setting myself up for failure but that wasn't an option for me. My argument was 'what parent would want to think smaller for their child?'. This I perceive to be my first rookie 'parenting' mistake - deciding for my "child" what their outcome would be before allowing them to take their own first steps and make their own decisions based on what is in their heart and not their parents' mind. The truth is that many parents do this with well-meaning intentions. They place enormous pressure on their children with little consideration for the impact it actually has when they don't live up to their parents' expectations.

Although I created a name for myself in the industry as the leading Kids Life Coach in the country, I was breaking inside. My heart was shattered into a million little pieces as my life took on a blur of over achievement and putting myself on a self-made pedestal. I replaced my pain with performance and my achievements brought me temporary reprieve as I was faced with the often-cruel remarks by clueless parents.

Like the time I was pushing a trolley with my mom in a local supermarket and an ex colleague of hers asked if she was a granny yet. When she replied not yet, the lady turned to me and asked, "What is wrong with you?" Of course, she did this tongue in cheek, thinking my husband and I had selfishly decided to abstain from being parents because of our careers. My response was to turn my back on her and walk away, leaving my mom to deal with the aftermath of trying to explain. It must have been just as hard for her but I am grateful that she has always been my buffer to the pain.

The reality of parenting
isn't always glamorous and that's okay

The franchise became a full time parenting job and with that, I lost part of my original purpose to make a real difference. I think so many parents may feel this. They have dreams for themselves and when their children come along, these are put on hold. These are truths never whispered out loud for fear of being cited as selfish. Then you get the opposite extreme in the parents who don't understand the value of self-sacrifice and forge ahead like I did in my business, regardless of the consequences and blind to who gets hurt in the process.

The amount of times I have heard parents complain about their children is too many to count. It starts with the little things that irritate them. Like having to wake up too early on weekends. Parent evenings at their children's school that are mandatory to attend. Yet another soccer match to get to on a cold blustery winter's day or another ballet recital. These complaints that have so often fallen on our ears as a childless couple, I would gratefully have chosen to pass our lips instead.

Parents just try to do their best with the resources they have available

I believe that many parents who complain about their responsibilities don't do so because they are malicious or filled to the brim with discontent. They are human and they falter in their resolve when life is busy and their schedule is jammed with appointments.

Yet, I cannot help but mention that I have noticed over my years of working with children, that those parents who are the biggest complainers are often those who enjoy their children the least. They miss out on the colourful rainbow of family life in-between the mundaneness of parenting. They fail to see the opportunities for building memories that last a lifetime and that will forever forge their family bonds to weather the storms of life together.

At this stage, I also have to give special mention to the casual, callous remarks I have heard from so many parents thinly disguised as self-professed child behaviour experts "You wouldn't understand, you don't have kids." These so called experts who self-nominate as knowing it all because they have conceived, are often raising their kids on hope and misguided experience alone.

They deem their sense of entitlement at being a parent to be the get out of jail free card that gives them permission to offend those that don't share the same experience. Often parents like this close their ranks to those who don't fit in. Needless to say, I have been on the receiving end of that many times and it happens more than you can imagine.

I am of the belief that parents can be classified into one of 4 groups when it comes to supporting their children.

Parent #1 is involved and will do whatever it takes to raise their children as solid contributors to society. They understand the value of coaching and see prevention and personal development as a way of life. They know that laying a solid foundation for mental well-being is best done in childhood and they choose a healthy lifestyle as a way to ensure this.

Parent #2 is aware of the external influences that impact on their child and whilst they try their best to put measures in place to support their children, they often only intervene once they see a visible problem needing attention. They are not scared to ask for help and they are willing to try new things if it meant their child will be the eventual winner.

Parent #3 is largely in denial and also very confused and overwhelmed. They are the ones who have been told by professionals, usually a teacher, that their child is displaying a problem either emotionally, socially, physically or intellectually. They are willing to do what it takes to help their child but are sometimes frozen in fear and indecision. Often I see these parents wait too late to intervene when things could have been largely prevented.

Parent #4 is the cause of their child's problems through a low functioning level of parenting. The tantrums, the arguing over bedtimes, bad eating habits and technology addiction are a result of their inconsistent interventions. This last type of parent is generally uninvolved usually their kids are the ones who end up making choices with an ugly outcome.

The truth is that the world of parenting is complex and scary to me as an outsider looking in. I have been lucky enough to have spoken to many parents who are such a breath of fresh air, who admit how scary the road is for them. I see them as brave and strong and realistic.

The parent who admits they need support is stronger than the parent who judges others because they might not feed their child organic fruit and vegetables instead of sugar laden fizzy drinks. They are also stronger than the parent who ignores the plethora of resources available but yet continue to struggle on their own for fear of being judged.

Parenting becomes simple when you realise your children don't need you to be perfect

So often I see problems in children that could be avoided simply by putting the basics in place. The 3 simple rules for parenting from this "mother of none" are what I reflected in my classroom as a teacher. They are based on what works in well-founded research on motivational theories and are so simple. Almost too simple. It doesn't take rocket science to get this and I don't need to be a parent to understand the benefits.

Children need boundaries.

Children need consistency and natural consequences in those boundaries.

Children need unconditional acceptance and forgiveness when these boundaries are overstepped.

It all seems pretty easy to me. As a 'mother of none' I practice these three simple rules in my relationships with every child I impact on and they work for me. I can't help but wonder why something lacking in unnecessary complexity isn't just implemented by parents as standard. I guess I will never know because this isn't something I can openly debate with parents who appear to get offended when a non-parent offers unsolicited parenting advice.

I have seen the complications caused in children because of dissent in the family and a lack of implementing the basics such as eating around the dinner table together or having regular fun together as a family. As a Kids Life Coach, I have seen the simple things that are lacking only because I am not in the story itself.

As parents, it can be hard to see the whole picture when you aren't sitting on the picture frame like I am. This is why in my Kids Life coaching program, I have designed a system where the child coaches the parent to get their needs met. All bad behaviour and problems in a child is a sign of an unmet need and it pains me that parents sometimes miss how easy those needs are to meet.

Like how far a simple "I love you" at bedtime can go. Or a hug at school drop off. A little note in the lunch box with words of praise. These daily affirmations plant the seeds of self-worth and lead to fulfilled kids who respect their parents and themselves in turn.

I can't avoid the fact that this exclusive "parents club" that has mostly refused to accept me and let me in, has fuelled my inadequacy as an adult and led to me doubting my career at times, even though I have a natural gift for coaching children.

It took me many years to realize that I am perfectly positioned to coach other peoples' children, simply because I have no other choice but to remain objective.

I see hope where parents see challenges. I never bring emotion into my Kids Life coaching because I have no frame of reference. This is what makes me so powerful at the work that I do. I have never argued with my own child over the mundane things that consume time and do little to foster relationships. I don't know what it is like to get frustrated when your child pushes your buttons because they want a reaction. So I just get on with things.

Children are the biggest blessing that parents sometimes take for granted without even realising

I am a proud aunty of five nieces and one nephew and they are the closest I have ever gotten to feeling that indescribable feeling that makes parents utter, "My kids are the best thing that ever happened to me."

Well, I wouldn't know, but what I do know is that my immense love for these six kids is the closest I will ever feel to being a parent. The love my nephew and five nieces give me back is unconditional and our relationship is solid simply because I am not their parent and so our dynamic is different.

I guess if we had children of our own, my husband and I would have invested our time into them, like all other parents do. But we don't. So we invest our time into the closest thing we will ever have and it gives us the greatest rewards. We are blessed.

If you are a parent, or thinking of becoming a parent or perhaps you are scared you may never become a parent like me, I want you to remember this: No matter your role, you will always benefit by placing yourself into somebody else's shoes.

Remove the blinkers from your eyes and use your inborn empathy to feel what others may be feeling. Don't judge that parent who gives in to their child's nagging for more toys. Stop playing judge to the parent who feeds their children junk food or lets them watch too much TV.

Remember that the hidden truths are often masked by adult inadequacies caused by the stunted development of their own inner child, that little child within each and every one of us adults that is yearning to come out and play.

In one way or another, we have all been damaged by our own parents. That is the truth. The one we dare not whisper out loud because we love those that have raised us.

The hidden truth is that parents will always get something wrong and will never be perfect. I believe that this is okay. I suppose this is easy for me to say, being on the outside looking in, but I truly believe that children and parents choose each other and that they teach each other worthy life lessons.

Children need to have a slightly uneven road surface because when it is too easy, they lose the room for personal growth. I think that parents are their children are each other's best teachers and that the 'family dance' has different tunes and different beats. For some, the music plays loudly and the dance is vigorous and intense.
For others, it is slower and more evenly paced, calculated and graceful. However, dancing is dancing, and as long as a parent and child are involved in the dance together, they will figure out the steps that best suit them. As long as love is the glue that holds it all together everything will always turn out okay.

The Hidden Truths behind Parenting:

- *If you don't fit into the status quo, be thankful because it means that you have something unique to offer the world.*

- *Running away from your problems just means that one day you will have to return and rip off the temporary Band Aid, which might be that much more painful.*

- *Decisions fuelled by ego are never sustainable. Being humble goes a long way in earning and maintaining respect from the children who are watching you.*

- *Never be scared of sharing your views even if it makes you feel vulnerable. You never know who may benefit, so give freely.*

- *Never give up on your life because of the voice inside your head. It is just a script that can be rewritten and you are the author writing the masterpiece of your life.*

- *Just because you believe something is true it doesn't necessarily make it true. Challenge your beliefs if they are holding you back in any way.*

- *Experience always trumps what is learnt in books, so apply yourself consistently and practice your skills until you become an expert at it.*

- *Your adversities are your biggest gift because they are moulding you for a greater purpose.*

- *You are a continuous work in progress and your happiness will eventually overflow into the lives of those around you.*

- *Children are easily influenced and often it is the shortfalls of their parents that cause their biggest behavioural challenges.*

2

KIDS IN THE ATTIC

Hidden Truth:
A teacher can make or break a child

As she lifted her skirt seductively and wriggled her way onto the lap of the boy with glazed eyes, I knew in that moment that I was out of my depth. In an inner-city London school my classroom was a dusty, dirty, discarded attic, testimony to the fact that the kids I was expected to teach were considered worthless. The seductive lap dance by this 11-year old girl made my heart break instantaneously and along with this, my confidence too.

I had been appointed as the supply teacher for a short-term position that involved getting the children to pass their numeracy and literacy exams. This seemed easy enough until I found out that the reason they were failing was tied to a complex web of circumstances that evaded my understanding. In my initial interview, nobody had told me that this position would involve so much more than simply getting them to learn. It was also about peeling back the layers of bad behaviour that held these kids back from their true potential.

Housed in what I now fondly call my temporary prison at the top of a derelict school, my previous teaching experience seemed fleeting and inconsequential. The layers of dust were evidence of the fact that nobody had entered this room for a while, and that it was simply a place to keep these children out of the way. I hastily concluded with my first glance around that old and neglected classroom, that, just as I had been told, these kids were unteachable.

If you had to ask me for an exact job description of what the principal expected me to do with these children during my short-term appointment, I suppose it would simply be classed as "baby sitter." Luckily, when accepting the role, I wasn't aware that no amount of studying, reading and experience could have prepared me for what was to come and that it was my passion for children that would see me through. Survival for me would come to mean pulling in the reins of these out of control children.

I was well aware of many teachers older and wiser and certainly more experienced than I was who would have found it perfectly acceptable to use bullying tactics to get them to submit, with scant respect for these children's dignity. For me this wasn't even an option and since I had never been a teacher that had abused my power and authority in that fashion, I didn't see myself starting then.

Bullying a child into submission through fear is never a sustainable solution

I remember wanting to be a teacher ever since I was a child of 6 years old, and with my mother being a school principal, I believe it was my destiny to follow in her footsteps. Little did I realise back then that I would be sitting in a foreign country just after the Twin Towers disaster having run away from my mainstream life because I couldn't have children of my own. I had baggage. Lots of it. So, on Day 1 of this seemingly insignificant supply teacher placement, I didn't realise that it was then that my destiny as a Kids Life Coach began to unfold.

Being ignored by the children and seeing them completely disengaged, I silently sat at my desk, just watching and listening and trying to make eye contact with as many of them as possible, simply just to connect on some level. I had used this tactic many times when teaching in top private schools in South Africa, where what I deem to be somewhat 'indulged' children would eventually settle down when they realised that I wouldn't start teaching until they were all making eye contact with me. In this case, I was stunned by the deafening reality of being ignored, and hearing those boisterous raised voices that showed me that these kids did not care at all about how long I sat and waited for them to calm down.

With no response at all towards me, not even a glimmer of interest, I knew that these kids: the marijuana smoking boy, the gang leader, the lap dancing minx - had all given up. They had decided to leave the status quo and use their bad behaviour as a shield from the realities they faced in life. I felt frustrated at the fact that these children struggled to learn because of their emotional baggage.

With their inability to enter the classroom without bringing along their feelings of shame, inadequacy, hurt and betrayal, they achieved poorly by traditional academic standards. It makes a great deal more sense when you look at a child's unreasonable poor performance and bad behaviour if you bear in mind that they are making choices and doing things based on what they have experienced as being done to them.

These children who had been labelled as "misfits, delinquents, intellectually inept "were not even teens yet, but their eyes told a different story, confirming that they were old beyond their years because of their circumstances. In Sociology, labelling theory looks at how the self-identity and behaviour of people may be influenced by the words used to describe or classify them.

In the case of these children, their behaviour resulted in the stigma of being unintelligent juvenile delinquents always getting into trouble. I saw first-hand how this powerfully negative label changed these children's self-concept and social identity. These children who lived in an urban area heavy with gangs, were sometimes even labelled by teachers in the school as gang members themselves even when they weren't.

Label the behaviour
not the child

I learnt the hard way that these kids were behaving the way they were, because it was what was expected of them. For so long they had been treated as worthless by the adults who were supposed to care for them that they had come to start thinking of themselves this way and so they stopped trying.

Some researchers believe that people of lower social status are more likely to be labeled deviant from the social norm and I can confirm that this appeared evident in the case of these children who lived below the breadline. They were neglected, and it appeared very much unloved and unsupported. To me, their behaviour was merely an expression of their inner turmoil.

After that first day of "teaching" what I had been told, and now also perceived to be, helpless and hopeless children, I went home and I cried. After my mini meltdown I had a hot bubble bath and soaked away my overwhelm. As I cooked dinner, which has always been my stress outlet, I stepped into problem solving mode because for me giving up was never a viable option. I put my resourcefulness into action and I stayed up all night, researching and formulating techniques to control these children's behaviour positively.

I use the word *'control'* loosely, because actually what I was after was to earn respect because I knew that with that came the enormous payoff of seeing these kids succeed. So many teachers like me on that day, understand the feeling of the classroom sometimes being a battle zone, forcing their backs against the wall with the children's complexities bearing down on them.

Building rapport is not about demanding perfection. It is about nurturing truth

Getting the majority of learners on your side in the classroom if you are a teacher is about building a rapport that centres around dignity. This is something easily taken for granted, with power and fear being asserted as the tools for gaining the upper hand. Behaviour management of any child is not about punishment, reacting or confrontation but it is about building a mutually respectful relationship.

I couldn't help but notice that the other teachers in the school had a very low regard for these kids and they treated them as guilty even before proven so. They simply had to be in the wrong place at the wrong time on the school field and they were deemed the instigators. This led to all sorts of other complex issues such as living up to their own self-fulfilling prophecy, which is a prediction that directly or indirectly causes itself to become true due to feedback between belief and behaviour. I was out to prove the judgmental teachers wrong. I was on a mission to uplift these kids and get the best out of them, something nobody prior to me had seemingly managed to do.

Day two of this supply teaching position brought with it a sense of anticipation as I came better prepared with an arsenal of new ideas. I consciously changed my body language that reflected me as meek and intimidated from the previous day, by stepping into Michelle Pfeiffer mode from my all-time favourite classroom cult movie, Dangerous Minds.

I didn't know then that I was actually striking what Amy Cuddy, a researcher at Harvard University, terms the 'power pose'. In her well known 2012 TED talk entitled 'Body Language changes who you are', she spoke about the impact body language has in relation to how you are perceived by others.

We make sweeping judgments and inferences about each other all the time from body language, and so my game plan to gaining the upper hand with these children was to fake confidence. I remember doing this day in and day out until eventually I actually came to believe it. I learnt to fake it till I became it. Whilst I don't recommend using this approach in the context of children, since they are pretty good judges of character and will eventually trip you up, it did work for me at the time. I am thankful for that grace in so many ways!

Define expectations
collaboratively with children
so that they feel a sense of ownership

That day, my newfound confidence started tweaking the curiosity of the kids, especially when I scribed a message on the black board behind my desk 'You can win a prize if...' Although the ring-leader of the class gave a running commentary about what he thought about my message, nobody really stopped to pay attention to me and the other kids simply nudged each other in curiosity. He held the power in that classroom and I realised that being in control is a basic force in every social interaction and that day he was the winner at his young age.

Power defines the way we relate to each other. It dictates whether you get listened to. It determines whether your needs take priority or get any attention at all. It was only when this intimidating young man with his untrusting eyes dropped his defences and showed an interest, that his followers got the opportunity to hear what I wanted to say.

This boy was actually what today is commonly termed a social bully because he often taunted the other children, appearing bold and confident on the surface but he was emotionally entangled in his own self-doubt. His brazen disregard for other peoples' feelings seemed to garner him the respect he wanted and sadly he was probably just mimicking the fear tactics other adults used on him.

I knew that with the undivided interest of the class in response to their ring leader's cue, I had a chance to orchestrate the carefully put together plan born in my desperate mind in the bubble bath and kitchen the night before.

"So what ya got to show us then?" said the tallest boy in the class, the one who would later come to be fondly known by the nickname of 'Smiley'. A deafening silence followed, with all eyes boring holes into my facade of me being a confident teacher.

In essence, I had very little experience, since I had only been teaching for less than 3 years. None of this experience was related to dealing with children who tested all semblance of normal boundaries. I sensed that that the kids felt a desire to peel away my skin and expose my vulnerability.

Being vulnerable is a gift
that connects people
through the heart and not the mind

I felt a twinge of guilt at that moment because my hastily scribbled words on the board weren't quite as perfect as they should have been for something so important. "My job", I said to the 10 sets of eyes staring at me, "is to keep you happy. When you are happy then I am happy. So, tell me, what would make you happy? Would winning a prize do the trick?"

When laughter erupted, I realised that I had been very optimistic about my audience. I had thrown them a life raft, but without giving it a chance, they were already drifting back out into their ocean of self-imposed helplessness. They had bigger things to worry about than winning a prize. Not to mention the fact that I had in a misguided way alluded to the fact that their happiness was my core objective and this was something I couldn't possibly promise.

These kids knew and felt little happiness, and defending their pride and dealing with circumstances such as prostituting moms, alcoholic fathers, gangs peddling drugs on every street corner being most important, they moved with uneasiness in their role of "adult" that life had cast them in.

When children are forced to grow up too fast, the side-effects show up eventually

The Centre for the Developing Child at Harvard University has done extensive early childhood research based on the biology of stress. They have found that major adversity, such as abuse, poverty, or neglect can weaken developing brain architecture and permanently set the body's stress response system on high alert. I saw this first hand in the mistrust these children treated me with because they saw me as just another threat.

It was a smaller boy that picked up the conversation from where the ring leader left off, his face hardened by what I was to later find out was a by-product of his mom prostituting her body outside his school every day. Whilst he was at school, she was selling her body to pay for the food that filled his tummy and the new trainers he sported on his feet, as well as to pay for her drug habits. A secret whispered to me by fellow teachers and not the boy himself so I am not sure how much was actually true.

He was lacking in confidence and could hardly keep eye contact, yet I could see something in him that wanted to be a winner. I learnt then that street law guides that when you have nothing to lose, surely you also have the chance of everything to gain with 50/50 odds. This child was taking the gamble as he said "Hey, hey guys. Let's give the little Missy a chance."

"So what ya got for us?", I remember him chanting insolently with a defiant stare in his eyes.

As I started explaining the reward system I wanted to implement, I seemed to feel what I can now only perceive to be a perverse sense of importance. I actually in my young inexperienced teaching mind believed that I was going to save these children. I wanted them to pass their numeracy and literacy exams so that I could prove how competent I actually was as a teacher. For me it was about gaining recognition and approval and the only way to do this was by demanding perfection from myself and them.

At that stage I still wasn't aware of the fact that the actual outcome I should have been looking for ways to give these kids the skills to deal with life long after I was gone. Since strong or negative emotions can be one of the biggest blocks to learning, the reverse is also true that for children to learn they need to be in a good emotional state.

We all learn emotional habits that can undermine our best intentions and this was what was happening here, but at first, I didn't see this. I was too naive to realise that there had to be a long-term solution available. I guess at the time I didn't know any better just like so many inexperienced teachers in classrooms around the world today. Doing their best with the resources they have available but not quite understanding the necessity for them equipping children with life skills as a priority rather than numeracy and literacy.

Being perfectly imperfect
is what unites us as a human race

With these imperfect kids, the reality did sink in somewhat that the chances were pretty low to gain the perfect results I so desperately wanted. "The prize," I said, "is a secret, and you can only find out what it is when you win it." It was then that the lap dancing girl with tight fitting school blouse who had seduced her class mate the day before, gazed at me in curiosity.

For her, keeping secrets was an everyday occurrence and the habit had become instinctual and deeply ingrained. She told me a few weeks later that her mom had taught her how to manipulate her body to seduce boys because it was the biggest weapon she had. She was only 10 when her first lesson in seduction occurred. Her mom had created the misguided truth in her that women have to use their sexuality to win men over. So, for her, my prize probably seemed pretty inconsequential in relation to her mom's promises of a life of being a fairytale bride, whipped away by a rich man if she practiced her lap dancing techniques.

"Would you like to know how to win the prize? All you have to do is let me catch you being good." As I made this ridiculous statement, my mouth was dry and I stumbled over my own words, my mind back peddling for a way out. *What had I been thinking? Did these kids even understand the definition of being good?* They probably understood being good as being street smart and able to cope amidst a life of turmoil and heartache. The lap dancing girl was good at seducing boys, the sexually abused twins good at hiding their secret, the boy with the prostitute mom good at pretending he didn't care.

Their lifeless eyes were rendered that way by life itself and being good was a perception I had created in my own mind. I feel embarrassed now that I actually used that word 'good' because if you look in the Oxford English Dictionary, you will see that it is comprised of 27 adjectives all underpinned by the desire to have the qualities of a high standard.

So actually, what I was telling these kids was that my expectations were high and that I expected more from them than they had given their other teachers. How unfair is it to expect children to live up to your definition of good before even building trust?

A teacher's perception of, and their response to their pupils' behaviours, are always at the heart of discussions about emotional and behavioural difficulties. My perception at that stage was that these were capable kids and that I expected them to behave as such. I guess my naivety was my undercover success catalyst in that classroom, and to this day I am thankful that I did not listen to those teachers who told me so many negative things about those children. I chose to leave the negative labels and vaguely accurate perceptions at the door and form my own opinions based on what these children showed me. In looking back, it was this sole act of trusting that these kids could do better and be better, that managed to transform their confidence levels.

Children attach importance to how you make them feel

Within days, my "caught you being good" initiative gained momentum as I rewarded every small effort made with an "entry ticket" to a lucky draw. If I saw somebody even attempting to lift a pencil to do some work, I gave them an entry ticket. If they said please or thank you, I did the same. When they let me enter the door before them or they smiled at somebody I rewarded them. This is what is commonly termed as extrinsic motivation which is related to modifying behaviour through the use of tangible rewards. This type of motivation arises from outside the child, as opposed to intrinsic motivation, which originates inside of the child.

At first, my intention was completely misguided and I realised that by rewarding them for the basics that I should have taken as a given and not an option, I was in essence making them focus on the prize and not the actual outcome.

I rewarded them for: getting to school, arriving on time, entering the classroom sensibly, having their school items with them, paying attention, listening to instructions the first time around, attempting to try even when something was hard, putting their hand up, talking and not shouting, sitting not slouching but most of all for treating each other with respect.

I did of course progressively make it harder to get the slips as they came to be conditioned like Pavlov's dogs who salivated every time he rang the bell even when the food wasn't there. They started thriving on the reward and the praise. Genuine praise I might add, that uplifted them and gave them a snapshot of their own self-worth in that dilapidated inner city classroom.

I realised that rewards per se had no long-term effect and probably wouldn't be the lasting predetermining factor to change their behaviour, however I could slowly see a sense of pride entering these children's lives as they tried harder each day to self-regulate and improve their own behaviour.

Give children the reassurance that life is about making good and bad choices

During each new school week, the kids would diligently and proudly post their slips of paper, bearing their name and why they had been "caught" into the brightly decorated box on my desk. At the end of each week, we would have a lucky draw and a prize would be awarded to one child. These prizes were small and varied from key rings to chocolates and they were very much valued by the winners of these rewards.

Initially, the children complained of unfairness when a peer, who didn't have as many slips won and they said that they hadn't worked as hard so didn't deserve the prize. I got their point, but explained to them that life was like that. In my experience, some people seem to have the knack for making less effort and getting the most external reward and recognition. This is a fact and is deeply rooted in the reality that they have simply learnt to work the system better.

The trick was for them to learn the euphoric feeling of their deep-rooted desires as motivational power such as having pride in themselves, self-acceptance, curiosity, honour, independence, order, social status and positive power. I wanted them to experience intrinsic motivation so that they would naturally, and without justification needed, want to perform a specific task. I wanted them to do this because their results fulfilled their desire to feel good about themselves and the importance they, and not somebody else, attached to it.

Gaining respect from others is about respecting yourself first

So often in life, we hide who we truly are, trying to impress others by being what they want us to be and behaving in a way that we think gains their admiration. I wanted more for these children who had spent so much of their young lives trying to "fit in". The irony is that their trying to fit in was a potential life sentence to a life of mediocrity. They were natural leaders and I simply saw myself as a catalyst to their personal development.

The biggest life lesson I was teaching them through my "caught you being good game" was that with more entries, you have more chances to win. Isn't it just so obvious that the more good we put into this world, the more good will come back to us?

The laws of reciprocity state that we do unto others what is done unto us. This translated into their lives in small ways at first: through them arriving at school on time, greeting each other in the mornings, handing their homework in, finishing classroom tasks on time, taking pride in their work. Later, as they became accustomed to the notion of "being good", their subconscious mind was actively seeking positive affirmations as a feel-good factor and not necessarily for the prize at the end of the week. The pay-offs were huge and our classroom became our home, where we united each day and shared and cared for each other.

The cold starkness of the fact I had no input into the choices they made when they stepped out of our haven of respite, did sometimes keep me up at night. I knew, though, that over the few months I had been their teacher, their minds had switched from victim to victor and that although life was hard for them, I could see that they now felt empowered to do more and be more.

Let your inner child out to play and watch the magic happen

I should mention that shortly after taking on this teaching position, I had realised that my initial assignment had been to simply remove these kids from their classrooms. I was the person tasked to "crowd control" them in a more insular environment, because they were being too disruptive during what is not very fondly known by teachers as SATS exams preparation.

This is the National Curriculum assessment that refers to the statutory tests carried out in primary schools in England. I learnt first-hand then, that the pressure on schools and teachers around the world to focus on measurement and comparisons of performance often obscures the interpersonal experience which should be at the heart of teaching.

When I went to the staff room during break times and tried to share my stories of my small successes, I was still met with some of the less caring teachers putting these children down. I wanted to stand on top of the highest mountain, shouting out, *"Just let these kids enjoy being kids! Stop labelling them as broken and stupid. Just teach them unconventionally and care for them unconditionally"*- an idealistic notion that has no place in a modern classroom, but it is what kept me going.

I have always been an idealist. I don't see life as black and white and my natural inclination to add colour to children's lives is a gift that I feel so blessed to have been given. The thought then, that I couldn't "fix" them, did occur to me multiple times throughout my time with these wildly spontaneous and misunderstood kids.

I couldn't take away their pain, nor feed their hungry tummies, nor give the ongoing love they were so desperate for. What replaced those initial thoughts of frustration was a powerful urge to equip them every day as best I could by coaching them to understand their own inner worth. This is where my love for coaching as a modality grew and it was the start of my later success in building a career based on what I learnt in the four walls of that classroom.

I grew to see my task as a teacher as simply being to immerse these children in a world where learning became fun again and to open up their imaginations and encourage them to be inquisitive in the safe space of our classroom.

As Socrates said, *"Education is the kindling of a flame, not the filling of a vessel"*, and that is what I set out to do with these kids. I made it my core objective to get them loving the notion of learning again. Since learning is a lifelong process, I saw this as a fundamental step in equipping them to reintegrate into their normal classroom when I was gone.

Maximise strengths rather than squander energy focusing on fixing problems

I remember how I sometimes got so frustrated when the kids came back to school after a weekend where their realities that consisted sometimes of things no child should bear witness to stepped in the way of their learning. My time in my classroom "prison" that consisted of discarded furniture, dusty windows and poor light, taught me more about myself than I thought possible. The seed was planted then for my life's work that I now commit my full time to, as an inspired contributor to children globally.

These broken children had allowed me to achieve what others had been unable to in a relatively short space of time, yet I still had the nagging doubt whether what I was doing would have a lasting impact. How could it when I was up against the dark forces of the adults in these children's lives who were messing them up? It was no secret that these children's parents were simply playing out what their parents had taught them and my hope was that I could somehow break that cycle.

I am proud to say that the children passed their exams and their behaviour significantly improved and along with this the perception of their teachers and other classmates. This was a dual carriageway and with the improvement of their own inner world attitude, their previously misguided energy was shifted in such a way that others noticed and started treating them more positively in return. Isn't this how we all are in life? We judge others based on previous behaviour, until they prove us wrong by consistently enacting their new more desirable behaviour.

I will admit that a lot of my success was about having a small class of only 10 children, which did give me the luxury of spending a chunk of the day tapping into the needs of these children that didn't reflect only in the pages of their numeracy and literacy books.

I had been given the luxury of getting to know these kids on more than a superficial level because we were a small and intimate group with the time to go beyond just traditional classroom teaching. This is why I teach my students who train to become certified Kids Life Coaches under my mentorship, to this day, that you should avoid the numbers in any group work being larger than 12. Mass motivation does little for long term success and the smaller you can keep it the better your results will be.

All bad behaviour is a sign of an unmet need

My initial 'caught you being good' reward system eventually fell away as I replaced it with a tailor-made approach geared towards each child's needs and strengths. Fundamentally, this is what coaching children is about - understanding that all bad behaviour is a sign of an unmet need, finding out what their needs are and meeting these needs.

I learnt how to really understand these children's needs and how they preferred me to express my appreciation to them. According to Dr. Gary Chapman, author of the book, 'The 5 Love Languages of Children', this can make all the difference in your relationship with a child.

He says that all children need adults to intentionally fill up their emotional love tanks. These children in my care had empty love tanks because of the neglect that was by far beyond their control with parents who had problems of their own. This is what made it hard for them to make good choices and which is why they defaulted to angry or acting out mode as the norm when threatened.

Although I was no substitute for their parents, I started filling these children's love tanks more effectively because I understood that without doing this, it would continue to be hard for them to learn.

Every one of us is individually wired to receive and understand love in different ways. So, it is important to discover when and how children feel loved. The 5 ways according to Chapman are: physical touch, words of affirmation, quality time, receiving gifts and acts of service. I used all of these, with the exclusion of physical touch since this went against the code of conduct in the school. Besides, with physical abuse by an adult being high amongst these children, I knew touch probably wasn't their core language anyway.

Bad choices don't have the monopoly on defining future potential

My purpose was cemented in that classroom as day by day, I saw the glimmer reappearing in those amazing children's eyes as I gave them the unconditional, unconventional, upbeat, uplift that they so deserved. The good news is that science shows that providing stable, responsive, nurturing relationships can prevent or even reverse the damaging effects of early life stress.

I would like to think that although I was with these children for such a small window of time, I left them with lifelong benefits for their learning, behaviour, and health. Through equipping them with the core skill of making positive choices, I can only hope that these children haven't ended up on the wrong side of the law or addicted to drugs like some of their parents.

My initial objective was to leave them happier than how I found them and I hadn't made them happy in the traditional sense, but what I had done was to give them the space to redefine themselves so that they could approach the world with a healthier outlook. The moment I believed in their inherent good and I didn't judge them for their past mistakes, they played to that.

If you want to achieve success when coaching children, this is one of the fundamentals you should apply. So many children are defined by their behaviour when it actually was never their fault to begin with. Although I don't blame parents, I do believe that neglect is one of the biggest contributors to the problems we are seeing in our 21st century children today.

I know now that I couldn't fix these children's worlds, I couldn't wrap them up in cotton wool to protect them, but what I did have the power to do was to educate, motivate and inspire them to embrace their circumstances with hope. Hope is not an ingredient that can be bottled or packaged but it is the key ingredient for a happy life. Hope is what keeps us going and allows us to be better, do better and have better. It feeds us with the strength to overcome our fears and to pursue our dreams.

In my brief time with them, I had coached these children to embrace hope and in return they had helped me to form my belief that every child deserves to have a coach to guide them through the stresses of life. I wish I knew where these children are today because I would personally thank each one of them for the lessons they taught me that paved the way for me building my global network of Kids Life Coaches.

Reality eventually shows up if you hide from the truth

After a two-year sabbatical from reality, and earning my stripes as a young teacher in a myriad of rough inner-city London schools, I returned to my country of birth, South Africa. I returned totally changed after my final teaching assignment with these amazingly talented kids, and I knew that I could never re-enter the teaching fraternity with the same outlook.

It is strange how the universe sends little sign posts to direct your attention. I remember returning to South Africa, still feeling empty because I wasn't a mother. I missed the children in the attic classroom, and I felt redundant once again, so I applied for a position teaching English in the same private school group I had previously taught at. I felt like I had no real purpose, and was searching for answers, so I enrolled in an evening course in philosophy at our local university.

At my first class, I remember a lady sitting opposite me in a horse shoe shaped seating arrangement. One of her chair legs was bending precariously inwards and looked destined to break. I pointed this out to her and we struck up a conversation. This lady later became my colleague. We eventually discovered that when I was turned down for the English teaching position, she was the one who was awarded the job instead of me!

This is one very relevant signpost I remember receiving from God. At the time, I was angry that this lovely lady had taken the job I had wanted, yet she was the one who highlighted that there may be an opportunity to land my dream job teaching Life Orientation to 9 to 12-year old's using my newly acquired London Toolbox.

Had I not met this lady with her broken chair leg, I would never have known about the teaching position. Thanks to her, I managed to develop an entire curriculum from scratch relating to what I had learnt to love the most in London - educating, motivating and inspiring children to live life with open arms and to shine their light into the world.

Pay attention to the sign posts in life that subtly point you in the right direction

This experience in the early stages of my teaching career was the next step of my love affair with learning all things related to motivating children. Seeing what a healthy dose of genuine interest did for these children inspired me to transfer this into engaging on a whole new level in my classroom moving forward. Most importantly, it also became the catalyst for 3 years later opening my Kids Life Coaching practice using the best parts of what these children and all the others before and after them had taught me.

I am thankful for my two years in England that started as a sabbatical from life, because it gave me a solid foundation without even realising it at the time. It led me to career prospects I could never have imagined.

Never underestimate the value of what children teach you and where it can take you. Use the lessons you learn to add colour to your future interactions and not only will you flourish, but the children you are in contact with will flourish.

The Hidden Truths behind Education:

- *No amount of studying, reading and experience can ever prepare you for supporting children. The key ingredient to coaching children is a genuine passion for having their best interests at heart.*

- *It makes a great deal more sense when you look at a child's unreasonable behaviour if you bear in mind that they are making choices and doing things based on what they have experienced as being done to them.*

- *Building a rapport centres around dignity. Behaviour management of any child is not about punishment, reacting or confrontation. It is about building a mutually respectful relationship.*

- *Practice walking your own walk and talking your own talk so that you become a role model that is respected for the real and not fake confidence you show.*

- *Many adults see being in control as a basic force in their social interaction with children. Exerting undue dominance over a child will result in their resistance. Give them a choice and they will willingly succumb.*

- *Many children who appear to be strong because they are bold and confident on the surface are usually emotionally entangled in their own self-doubt.*

- *Strong or negative emotions can be one of the biggest blocks to learning, so for children to learn, they need to be in a good emotional state.*

- *Immerse children in a world where learning becomes fun by opening up their imaginations and encouraging them to be inquisitive.*

- *Coaching children is about understanding that all "bad" behaviour is a sign of an unmet need and it is your responsibility to find out what their needs are.*

- *Believe in children's inherent good and don't judge them for their past mistakes. Hope is what keeps children motivated even when faced with tough circumstances because it feeds them with the strength to pursue their dreams.*

3

TAKING A BATH IN COLD JELLY

Hidden truth:
Children are braver than adults

You know that feeling when you meet somebody that you instantly connect with? This was that kind of moment and one that I would remember for the rest of my life. She was beautiful in personality and she shone with the pure radiance of a human who was completely oblivious to the label that life had placed on her. She was classed as different, in a "special" school for kids who were intellectually and physically challenged. I thought she was perfect just the way she was and she taught me the most beautiful life lesson that is imprinted on my heart and mind forever. The best part is that, as a young adult, she is now my friend.

Being 12-years old at the time of meeting her for the first time, it was unusual to hear her asking me, "Do you like hugging?" Before I could even take a breath to answer, she had enveloped me in her small arms with her cerebral palsied hand.

"Wow. She's a hugger everybody. She's a hugger. Make way for the small girl with the world's biggest hug. Sheeee'sss a hugger!", I chanted in the silly voice I reserved for entertaining the kids I coached. She beamed at me with obvious pride because I was so impressed with her warm personality.

We both slumped onto the bean bags in my newly kitted out coaching space. The paint was still fresh and pungent and my colourful polystyrene wall decorations were a jovial backdrop as we burst out laughing. "I think we are going to get on just fine!" "Just fine." She repeated after me.

Her mom stood a short distance away with a knowing smile on her face. Obviously, she had seen this reaction to her daughter before. I was in awe of how self-assured and loving this stunning child with a physical and mental disability was. She radiated hope in every sense of the word and I could tell that although mom had come to me with a minor problem, it would all turn out okay.

Being fearless can have a downside if boundaries aren't in place

"So, beautiful girl, do you know why mommy has asked me to speak to you?". A moment of hesitation and then, "Ummm, because I need to learn how to stand up to the boys? Am I in trouble?", she asked.

In a dual medium school for mentally challenged children, the one thing that wasn't stunted were the hormones pulsating in harmony with their entry into adolescence. They may have been labelled as slightly slower in brain capacity, but nature still had her own time-table and the children in this special needs school developed just as any normal teenager would.

"In this space," I said reassuringly, "there is no such thing as being in trouble. I am here to make your brain stronger so that you can say no to those silly boys that might want to date you."

In our initial conversation, her mom had seemed paralyzed by her helplessness and fear that her daughter would fall prey to horny teenage boys who would coax her gentle nature into doing things she may not want to do.

"Everybody loves my daughter," Mom stated proudly. "She is one of those kids who sees the world as a beautiful place and trusts people with unwavering loyalty." In initial conversations with parents, when they describe their child's dilemma, I tactically leave a pause in the air to allow time to regroup. In this particular case, I commend mom for being so forward thinking.

"I don't want to wait until things go wrong before I do something. What if she….". Her words trailed off, leaving an unease in the air. I had only been in the Kids Life Coaching game for a year and this was my first situation like this. My head was scrambling for the right words, because I didn't know how I was supposed to answer a question that wasn't actually a question.

Assertiveness training is what Hugging Girl needed, but there I was struggling to assert my professional opinion and reassurance coherently. I had never coached a child labelled with mental and physical deficits before and I had my reservations that my programme would even work for her.

"I promise you that you have nothing to worry about." As I said it, I immediately heard that condescending little voice in my head telling me in no uncertain terms that I was not telling the truth. How could I possibly make a promise that was out of my reach and most certainly out of my control? Well, I had said it, and being a person of my word, and of course with my professional integrity at stake, I made a vow that I wouldn't let Hugging Girl and her mother down.

Sometimes trusting the process is what makes all the difference

It was the most fun I had ever had in all of my years as a Kids Life Coach. Our sessions were punctuated with loud giggles and lots and lots of talking. Boy, oh boy, she never stopped talking, coupled with lots and lots of hugging and giggling. Our productive conversations were so frank and honest that they taught me lessons that to this day stick in my mind. The biggest of which includes how easy it is to love unconditionally when you have no expectations in return.

In line with her mother's biggest fear of her falling prey to teen boys, in our third coaching session, we started practicing assertive communication skills. This involved a lot of role play and she took to it like a duck to water. She was by no means stupid and her aptitude for learning and retaining information was commendable. She embraced all that she learnt with open arms and she turned out to be one of the most diligent children I have ever had the privilege of coaching.

I still remember it so clearly, during that communication skills coaching session, how we were speaking about fears, and she proudly claimed that she was scared of nothing. A noble notion, but one that could have the potential to get her into trouble in the years to follow.

In line with my coaching policy of sharing myself authentically and being a realistic role model to children, as I discussed the topic, I shared with her that I had a fear of heights and of snakes. I had always been scared of heights. I still don't know how it happened or why it happened, but on a subconscious level it was so deeply imprinted that when exposed to a potentially "harmful" height related situation, my body would immediately go into fight or flight mode. My heart would bounce out of my chest and my hands would become balls of sweat as my mind was fighting with every ounce of dignity to not give in to the immense need to keep myself safe.

I had never shared this with anybody in detail, yet that day I chose to tell my story. This led to the unfolding of events that were to cement my belief that children can teach us more than we teach them.

All children are natural teachers bringing lessons to remind adults what really counts

"I am so very scared of high things that I would rather take a bath in cold jelly," I declared. Her response: "I love eating jelly and I love climbing high things."

Well, who was I to argue with that notion? It was then that she came up with the idea that was the catalyst for a chain of events that would forever banish my fear of heights- simply because she chose to challenge me to push myself to my own limits. She shared her story of climbing an indoor climbing wall that was 22,5 metres tall. Not once, not twice, but multiple times. With her physical disability one would have assumed that this would be an impossibility, but she saw her climb as a mighty success, and she explained how much she loved the adrenalin rush it gave her.

My coaching had clearly worked, because I had a young girl who was in return gifting me with her insight, wisdom and knowledge on a topic she enjoyed and loved. One of the indicators of reaching success in my coaching programme, is when children take what you have instilled in them and begin to coach others. She did just this that day, proving to me that I had laid a foundation for her future assertiveness and success.

Her words were simple and are tattooed on my mind forever: "I can coach you to not be scared."

She proceeded to explain in a lengthy and animated conversation how she had climbed to the top of this indoor rock structure and how she could show me how to do the same. I looked at her cerebral palsied hand with skepticism but I saw the determination on her face and soon realised just how serious she was about helping me overcome my fear.

"I would love you to coach me", I boldly declared when she really became persistent about the fact that she was going to be my Life Coach.

That day, when mom arrived to fetch her from our session, she pounced on her explaining with vigour that I 'wanted" to go and climb the rock with her. Well, this is not quite what I had said but at that late stage, I was prepared to roll with it, secretly hoping it would fizzle out.

Face your fears because you want to, not because you have to

So, every time I saw Hugging Girl for coaching over a time frame of 3 months, we ended our coaching session with her sharing her wisdom and insights into how to climb this massively tall structure without being scared! She even coordinated a date with her mom and insisted that she bring her camera to record the momentous occasion.

Well, let me tell you, when I realised how serious she actually was, I sneakily tried to manoeuvre my way out of our arrangement. I openly expressed this through my vulnerability in the hope that I could quietly remove myself from this predicament I found myself in.

"I am not scared of high things anymore!", I announced in one of our coaching sessions, with a convincing tone that was shadowed by inner self doubt. "Thank you so much for coaching me to be brave!"

She gave me an uncharacteristic glare, one that I had not seen before on her usually friendly face which only ever radiated love and beauty. Her look cemented the fact that my back pedalling was not going to go the way I thought it would. She embarked on a mini "lecture" that left me with a deep red flush spreading over my chest as it always did when I became anxious.

"You are not giving up", she announced, sealing the deal with, "You can come and climb the rock wall with me. I will ask mommy if she can fetch you." My carefully orchestrated attempt to extricate myself from this situation did not do the trick and she became more and more persistent that we were to achieve this giant feat together.

"You have to use your brain to tell yourself you can do it. Just imagine yourself climbing the rock. Tell yourself you can do it." This became the weekly mantra that this precious girl recited to me. Slowly but surely, with her sincerity and belief in my ability, I started enjoying the process and participating in her "guided" visualisations where I saw myself reaching the pinnacle of this indoor climbing structure harnessed in safety ropes and safely abseiling to ground zero after my summit!

Facing scary things accomplishes self-mastery

In no time at all, the date we had planned to climb together slid into view and it was time to embark on our crazy and exciting excursion to conquer 'The Rock'. My resolve was solid and my fear had seemingly been banished by my months of coaching from this precious child. Yet what was to happen next, I couldn't have anticipated.

On the day, all harnessed up and ready to start our ascent, my body took control of my mind. I could feel little droplets of nervousness escaping my armpits and dripping off my forehead. I was in trouble and my body was slowly going into overdrive, with my mind chastising me for even getting into this situation.

Fear of heights or acrophobia is a debilitating anxiety disorder that affects nearly 1 in 20 adults and I was one of them. My symptoms of the fear were in excess of what the actual situation was and I felt a rising panic and anxiety that was hard to control. If you have ever had a fear, you will know what I am talking about when I mention muscle tension, headaches, panic attacks, palpitations, or dizziness.

A full-blown panic attack resulting from the fear of heights can cause breathlessness, loss of control, and even thoughts of dying. I had only ever felt that way once before when I flew overseas on honeymoon and almost crushed my husband's hand. Luckily, since that day, most of the time, my two feet were planted firmly on solid ground, but in front of that "rock" I felt like I was having an out of body experience.

I seemed to have no control over my mind and it resisted the challenge with all its might, sending red flags that I shouldn't go ahead. Despite my body signalling that all was not well, I knew that I simply had no choice but to follow through.

I was fully engaged in the fight or flight response which is the body's natural response to perceived threat or danger. My adrenalin was released and I could feel my heart rate speeding up, and consequent perspiration releasing because of it. My acute stress response is something you may have experienced yourself, and it refers to a psychological reaction that occurs in the presence of something that is terrifying, either mentally or physically.

I think the body is pretty amazing actually and this is one of the things that I coach children to understand- that in a stressful situation, a chain of rapidly occurring reactions inside our body help mobilise our resources to deal with threatening circumstances. In response to acute stress, the body's sympathetic nervous system is activated because of the sudden release of hormones. The sympathetic nervous system then stimulates the adrenal glands triggering the release of adrenaline and noradrenaline. This results in an increase in heart rate, blood pressure and breathing rate. After the threat is gone, it takes between 20 to 60 minutes for the body to return to its pre-arousal levels. For me that day, I am sure it took longer!

Know the difference between
fear and anxiety

I want to be clear here that although I had a fear of heights, this wasn't the emotion I was experiencing that day. Fear is the emotion you experience when you are actually in a dangerous situation, and I wasn't. Anxiety is what you experience leading up to a dangerous, stressful, or threatening situation and during the said event.

If you have ever taken a ride on a roller coaster, you will understand the difference between anxiety and fear. Anxiety is what you feel when you are in the line waiting for your ride, as you watch the loops and steep drops, and hear the screams of the other riders. You also probably feel anxiety when you go on the roller coaster and every time you get closer to the top of the first drop or hill. Fear is what you experience as you go over the peak of the hill and start your fall.

Reaching the top is about ignoring the distractions and looking upwards

With this in mind, I felt like I was on a roller coaster, but instead of the fear, I felt anxiety that overwhelmed my senses. All the coaching this young girl had done with me had worked at the time, but my body and mind had other ideas.

With all the courage I could muster, I announced, "Okay, I'm ready. I can do this", more to myself than anybody else. I might add that I sounded so in control to the people watching that I almost convinced myself that all would be okay.

I had to hide my fear and emotions at all costs. I was a role model and an example to Hugging Girl and I did not have the luxury of falling apart. My spell of momentary bravery was broken by a well-muscled young man doing a safety check. I realised in rising horror that I was going to scale a wall vertically using small stepping stones as grips for my hands and feet. I was mortified at the fact that in the lead up to my climb, a small crowd of watchers had gathered as the Hugging Girl by my side joyously announced what was about to happen. Her mom was in tow, diligently recording the moment for eternity on her camera.

So, I did what I needed to do. I put on my big girl panties (well actually it was a very unflattering harness) and started climbing.

My stylish French manicured nails were no match for the climb and they were ruined within minutes as I frantically fought for gripping space whilst scaling the wall.

With consistent encouragement, I could hear Hugging Girl's voice - a beacon of light in the sea of overwhelm that was threatening to drown me. "You can do it Zelna. Think of the top of the mountain.

Use Zeal Talk." (This is one of the tools I had given her - the use of positive affirmations to self-encourage).

I cannot describe the feelings I had because they were an unnaturally blended combination of fear and awe. I looked at her then with great pride in my eyes, as she clambered up the steep incline with a hand and a leg that were compromised by her physical disability. She was slow and careful as she climbed, setting the pace for us to complete this challenge together as a team.

Then disaster struck. My fight or flight mode kicked in with a vengeance, determined to stop my mission. "I can't do this anymore. I got halfway, now I'm going down." I said. For a momentary glimpse, the look in her eyes was one of disappointment which transformed almost immediately into a smile.

"Just look at the top, Zelna. Keep climbing. We are almost there." I tried so hard to be brave, but tears welled up and trickled slowly down my flushed cheek. I didn't even have a free hand to wipe them away with and so I decided in that moment that I was going to keep going, not to save face, but so that I didn't disappoint this angel who had so lovingly encouraged me over the past few months.

I remember that moment of reaching the top. Yes! The very top! The very very top part that had seemed so insurmountable. In a record breaking half hour of agonising persistence, I had faced my fear and conquered my anxiety. "Yeah, we did it!", we chanted together, focused only on the accomplishment we felt in that moment. I was exhausted but swept up in the warm glow of euphoria. Then I glanced down.

"Ummmm, so how do we get down?". After having a few dodgy experiences on past teen leadership camping expeditions, the abseiling part didn't appeal to me at all. Gripping so tightly to the rock that my knuckles whitened, I diligently tried to convince myself to make the descent. Luckily for me, the well- muscled boy joined us and eventually skillfully led us back to solid ground.

The innocence of children
makes them good teachers

The reason this was such a major accomplishment is simple. I was an educated, accomplished professional with a fully functioning body and mind. Hugging Girl was still learning, and labelled with a disability in both her body and her mind. She took my confidence to new heights through her encouragement. This is a simple illustration that as adults we need to explore a child's potential by sharing their strengths and not focusing on their perceived weaknesses.

There is no reason why a child cannot be an accomplished teacher to an adult, and I believe that it is only when we truly start listening and learning from those younger than us, that our world will be healed. That we as adults will be healed.

Be willing to learn and grasp new lessons with a child-like thirst

Many years later, Hugging Girl is now a young lady, and she and her mom are still very much a part of my life. We see each other occasionally as friends rather than clients, and the impact they have left on my heart and my confidence is testimony to the fact that you should never underestimate somebody's ability because they are not part of mainstream schooling or able to hold down a 9 - 5 job.

Today, Hugging Girl is accomplished and loved and respected by all that know her. It doesn't take being whole in the traditional sense to make an impact on those around you. What it takes is sharing the best parts of yourself that you have to give - taking the time to talk, to love, to connect and to care just like she did in my life.

Our lives are becoming more and more frantic and with this hustle and bustle we have become desensitised to what really counts. The majority of adults have become trapped in their minds rather than living with their hearts. They have forgotten what it means to play, and to just be, rather than to always be in control and doing.

I know firsthand how I grew personally with my accomplishment of participating in and completing a challenging task with Hugging Girl. I was scared, but she inspired and encouraged me and she has left me with a great story to tell.

I want to ask you, what is it that you fail to see in yourself? What aren't you hearing about yourself? What can children teach you that will catapult you to your full potential? You see, as adults we are still learning beings who need to grasp certain lessons and it is naive to think that none of these will come from children.

As a Kids Life Coach, I have experienced my most profound personal growth in the sessions where I have seen the resilience and determination of children who have every reason not to succeed. Even with the odds stacked against them, they show commitment to the process rather than the outcome. They are trusting and non judgemental.

Resigning yourself to mediocrity means giving up with your song still inside you

Adults on the other hand, carry their baggage around with them like a prize that is worthy of recognition. They make excuses and place limitations on their own abilities. I am no exception to this rule. I often have to remind myself that I hold myself back because of limiting beliefs that can be easily reprogrammed. I am a constant work in progress and so should you be. If you want to be a role model to children, you need to constantly push your boundaries and exert your limits. Take on challenges that stretch your mind, but most of all, that leave a story to tell like mine.

Participate in a marathon, go shark cage diving or hike up a mountain. Whatever it is you choose to do, just do it for yourself. Don't do it to gain recognition or to prove a point, but genuinely model your desire to better yourself so that children can follow in your footsteps. So many adults resign themselves to mediocrity purely because they accept their fate as written in stone.

They see no other way and so relax themselves into the mundane existence of a daily life that is devoid of passion and energy. What a waste. What a terrible tragedy that so many children are destined to that same fate if we don't intervene.

Adults need to take control and to share their fears with children. Whisper those secrets of yours out loud so that children can be inspired when you come out on the other side. Work through your limitations with vigour and the strength that encourages children to do the same.

I remember going to a water park with my nephew who at the time was 7. He was terrified of going down a particularly daunting water slide and as we stood in the queue to reach the top, I coached him. I told him how scared I was too and I relayed my story of Hugging Girl.

I explained that it was normal to feel fear and it was in these moments that there is the potential to experience our greatest achievements. By the time we got to the top of the slide, he was so psyched up that with a smile on his face he turned to me and said, "Let's face our fears together Aunty Zelly."

I had given him permission to be scared without judgement and through showing him my fear, he had mustered up the strength to take the plunge with me. At one stage he had wanted to turn around and walk back down the steep stairs, but he didn't because I told him I needed him to help me. We still speak of that event as a great accomplishment for both of us.

Feeling uncomfortable is good if you use it as a learning opportunity

Why is it that we deem ourselves as the all-knowing and all perfect ones as adults? We also get scared. We also have fears. We also have anxieties. This is part of life and nothing that cannot be overcome when the right tools are utilised.

Children, on the other hand, are naturally brave and don't see the danger like we do. In fact, they run directly into danger without a second thought of repercussions. Like the time I took a group of learning-disabled children on a weekend camp with my husband and mom in tow for added supervision.

My husband spotted a snake which at the time we didn't know was harmless and when he pointed it out, the children ran towards it to take a closer look rather than away from it and to safety.

The reason is that children are spontaneous, and risk is an essential component of a balanced childhood. Exposure to healthy risk, particularly physical, enables children to experience fear, and to learn the strengths and limitations of their own body.

In this age of helicopter parenting that protects children from just about everything, there is a lack of opportunity for children to flex their risk perception muscles.

We need to give our children real childhoods that are not backed up by countless hours playing simulated games in isolation in a darkened room on an electronic device. They need to be outdoors.

Climbing, exploring and playing. They need to be exposed to a space where scrapes and grazes, falls and panic are normal. This way their risk radar can be adequately activated and they can start making choices for themselves based on what they feel is safe rather than on what adults tell them they should or shouldn't be doing.

Over protected children have great difficulty in building confidence when it comes to taking on new tasks. It is only in allowing children to conquer their perceived fears without adult interference that we give them the opportunity to flourish. Anxious parents breed anxious kids and, in a world, where there is realistically a lot of danger lurking on every corner, there is an even greater risk of children losing touch with their inherent ability to assess how realistic these dangers are.

So, in facing my fear of heights, with beautiful Hugging Girl, my next task is to muster my inner courage and jump out of an aeroplane - with a parachute of course! (Watch this space…I'm not promising but can only hope).

I want to take myself to the next level and push myself out of my comfort zone. I no longer go into adrenal shock when I think of it and I have been working on harnessing my mind power for success.

We need to do the same for our children. By pushing themselves to constantly grow into a new challenge they will develop the mindset of success. Getting ahead in life, isn't about mastering the easy things, it is about overcoming the difficult things with bravery and strength. It is in these times that the greatest lessons can be found.

The Hidden Truths behind fear:

- *Always be willing to learn and grow in the company of a child. It is in admitting your own fears that they will feel empowered to overcome theirs.*

- *A child who is labelled due to a perceived deficiency is also worthy of respect. Their disability often disguises our greatest opportunities for understanding humility and persistence.*

- *Our biggest lessons can be found in our hardest challenges. When we conquer these, the accomplishment is our best teacher.*

- *Overcoming what we fear is a catalyst for personal growth. The sense of achievement is a tonic for building confidence that will take you to the next level after that.*

- *Protecting children from dangerous situations does not mean cocooning them in a protective shield. It simply means teaching them to assess danger realistically.*

- *Children will get hurt in life. This is unavoidable but also essential for flexing their risk perception muscles.*

- *Ask yourself what is on the other side of that fear. If you don't know the answer, be brave enough to go and find it.*

- *Often when you begin to question a scary feeling it cannot be validated and so becomes redundant as a result.*

- *Children are naturally curious and they learn through exploring. Allowing them to do this with the risk of getting hurt is hard, but also very valuable.*

- *Over protected and sheltered children struggle to build resilience and confidence relating to tackling new challenges.*

4

CONDOM BOY

Hidden truth:
*Parents sometimes make bad choices
that mess up their kids*

He was barely a teenager, but he was an old soul, with wisdom beyond his years. His brother, scrawny and unable to hold eye contact, sat expectantly beside him.

"Mom put food on the table for us. My job was to stay away from the flat and look after my brother." The ginger haired boy stared at me intently, his gentle wave of freckles distracting me from the pain in his eyes.

"Sometimes she would run out of condoms, and that was also my job. I would go to the Family Planning clinic and fetch some for her. She had no time to waste. 'Time is money' she always said."
My mouth must have gaped open wide because he hurriedly said to me, "Don't worry, I told them they were for me so that mom didn't get into trouble." In my mind, I was fighting the urge to say out loud *How could the nurses believe you? You are only 12!*

In my mental archives, I needed validation for the nurses behaving so irresponsibly so I took it upon myself to google the words "Youngest School Girl Pregnancy". I want to caution you that unless you want to be shocked, don't take a look at the Wikipedia list that I found, where the youngest girl to give birth is listed as age 5 from Peru in 1939. It is unknown as to who the father is. Or so they report.

I am horrified at the statistics I have read that point to the fact that so many young girls are sexually abused, sold into marriage and raped. No wonder condoms were so willingly being handed out to juveniles without follow up, especially in a country like South Africa where the population is exploding.

I then did the same search for "Youngest School Boy Father" just to appease my conscience. Most of the information I found was in sensational news reports telling stories of pre adolescents, fathering babies with their girlfriends the same age or younger than they are. It always seems more dramatic when a girl falls pregnant, but this boy having such easy access to condoms could have been construed as a good thing or a very bad thing.

It took a short while for me to regain my composure to remind myself of the reason why the two brothers were sitting in front of me. Thanks to a generous corporate donation I had been approached and task forced to work with a children's shelter. On my first visit there, I was struck by the colourful curtains and the children playing in the yard on swings. What I didn't see however was adult supervision that convinced me the children were in good care. Yet, they all seemed happy and content. They seemed well fed and had a roof over their head.

I couldn't help but feel that something was amiss but at the time couldn't put my finger on it. I now know that my gut intuition was right. At the time, I had no idea that Condom Boy and the other children that I would work with, were potentially the victims of a child trafficking scheme that would later be unveiled on a major investigative journalism programme. This ended up in the founder of the charity out on bail and spending 4 years in court for the allegations, with the charges eventually being dropped because of lack of evidence and the disappearance of witnesses.

The truth means different things to different people

"I know you have been through a lot, but when you step into this room, you get to leave that all behind. Here we speak about your future and you get to move forward with me by your side," I stated, in the most empathetic tone that I could muster under the circumstances.

Condom Boy stared at me as if to say *'Are you kidding me?'* The venting that was to follow my naïve comment was filled with venom, heartache and blame. "My mom was a bitch, but she was my mom. She put food on our table by having sex with men. Sometimes they would touch me in my private place you know." His words flowed out of him like a dripping tap, now turned on and free to flow.

Without pausing for breath or having consideration for time, he told me his story. What I heard that day, permeated the safe space of my brightly coloured Kids Life Coaching space and turned it momentarily into a dark, sombre place that now held truths that I had long been avoiding. I didn't want to hear nor accept the ugly side of childhood because I didn't know how to deal with it.

I was highly sensitive to children's pain and I absorbed it as my own, a trait not always suitable for a Kids Life Coach, so avoiding the truth suited me just fine. On that day, I was forced to hold my stare with the monsters that lived in this boys mind, and it reminded me why I had chosen to be a coach and not a psychologist.

I remember a time where I wished I had the opportunity to do a degree in Child Psychology instead of a Bachelor in Education Degree. The fact is that at the time of making my career choice, going to University was a costly affair and I was offered a full bursary to become a teacher instead.

So in essence my destiny was mapped out for me because of circumstance and I am now grateful for this. Little did I know that this bursary would not only be one of my biggest financial gifts but it would also change the course of my career unimaginably.

I often get asked what the difference is between what a child psychologist does and what a Kids Life Coach does? I will tell you one fundamental difference that underpins the core philosophy, and that is that it appears that I get to have more fun!

When your work becomes your play, you know you have mastered sharing your gifts

As a Kids Life Coach, I describe my work as playing for a living! Now don't get me wrong, I am not saying that child psychologists don't have fun, but what I am saying is that as a Kids Life Coach, I reframe problems that children are faced with and use practical right-brained activities and tangible tools that children love to participate in.

There is a time and place for a child psychologist and I work alongside them in various scenarios, particularly when a child has undergone severe trauma like these two boys.

Most psychologists work with children to diagnose conditions and provide counselling and therapy. They may evaluate children for a variety of disorders or developmental delays, and they help children overcome abuse and other experiences that have impacted negatively on their mental and emotional health.

A child psychologist and a Kids Life Coach complement each other and although our eventual outcome is united in that we want a child to be a fully functioning adult, as a coach, my focus is on the here and the now. I don't look at the past and try to deconstruct what has gone wrong. I don't listen to hours of traumatic stories that drain the child emotionally, leaving me feeling helpless in that I can't do more to ease the child's pain. I empower children by focusing on the solution by setting clear goals within a predetermined time frame.

My intention for these two boys was for them to leave my sessions equipped with a toolkit of transferrable skills that they could practice on a daily basis. You can't expect meaningful change to happen in a child if you see them once a week for an hour, so I focus on what happens when the child isn't with me in my coaching space and I make it my priority that they will know how to cope.

Working in collaboration is a winning formula

In the weeks that followed, I coached Condom boy and his younger brother alongside the psychologist and the social worker who had been assigned to their case. As I said, there is a place for therapy and coaching to work hand in hand when a child is under severe emotional strain.

I was able to equip these boys by supporting them in solving problems and moving forward in life. Their emotional trauma was severe and their appointed psychologist did fantastic work helping them to process and externalise what had happened to them.

My job was to give them a snapshot of possibility and hope. I encouraged them to think big and remove the shroud of negativity that encompassed their lives. They got to just be kids and I coached them to understand how their brains work and how to create the life of their dreams.

Now removed from their once 'adult world', they were becoming kids again. Slowly, slowly they started smiling more, and were spontaneous with sharing stories about their new school and the friends they had made. My hopes were on a steady incline and I was seeing potential in these boys that outstripped their harsh start to life. Then the wheels fell off. Unannounced and unexpected.

Sometimes when the wheels fall off it means they didn't fit properly in the first place

I got the call from his social worker that Condom Boy had been excluded from his school. Each week, the social worker had been keeping me up to date and I was fully aware of his repeated run ins with his teachers, so I knew that the final straw had to be something big. It turns out, it was way bigger than big.

The underlying catalyst was his illiteracy compounded by his missed schooling. He was failing dismally on an academic scale and the other kids were calling him stupid. The teachers had done nothing to support him in this bullying, and their inaction eventually, in my opinion, led to the final outburst of him breaking the nose of one of his perpetrators in one swift punch.

Unfortunately, as so often happens in formal education, teachers have a habit of comparing siblings and their achievements. When one doesn't measure up to the other, they label the lack of achievement as laziness or a bad attitude.

They compared Condom Boy to his younger brother, who was in comparison bright as a button. He was also popular, confident and witty. This came from the cocoon of protection his older brother had always provided him. All the years of protecting his younger sibling from the harshness of the reality that was their life, had finally taken its toll.

On the day of his explosion, leading to the controversial but probably well-deserved injury, his teachers had rubbed too much salt in his wound of being dim and apparently stupid. So, his fuse was short and after hearing it all day from the teachers, all he wanted was peace during break time. When he didn't get that, he lashed out. Understandably so.

I don't advocate violence in any form or fashion but this boy had been pushed too far. Not only was he previously a victim of abuse at home, but this now translated into his classroom and also onto his playground. It was sad to watch him shrivel into himself after that incident and I had to work hard to get him back to the level he had been at. Building his confidence was a priority, and this started from within. I was unable to change his circumstances, but I could equip him to change his thoughts.

Usually when a child is negative about their self-worth, this translates into their external environment as bad body language, lack of eye contact, slouching shoulders or a dishevelled appearance. Condom Boy had all of the above and just by looking at him, you could tell he was vulnerable, which made him easy pickings for those wanting to find a scapegoat to elevate their own feelings of self-worth.

Falling apart at the seams while nobody is watching happens more often than you think

I coached him on maintaining a good posture and how to hold somebody's stare with confidence. What it meant to brush his teeth and hair every day and wear clean clothes. These things seem so basic, but they changed his life in a small way. Through respecting himself, he started seeing a change in how others respected him.

I won't lie to you. It wasn't an easy journey but it was worth every bit of time I invested in him. On the flip side, I worked on his younger brother's over confidence and his reliance on always having his older brother fight his battles for him. Both of them grew tremendously simply because I was paying attention to them and giving them the time they so needed after years of neglect from their prostitute mother.

On a weekly basis, I used to visit the shelter where the two brothers lived, to interact with the rest of the small group of kids that ranged in age from 4 to 12. I got to know them and they took me for tours of their "bedrooms", which were tiny boxes set up in dorm like style, cheaply and cheerfully decorated. Perfectly comfortable, but dulled at the edges and certainly not a homely space for children.

I met the charitable founder of the shelter on more than one occasion and at the times that I did, there was always awkwardness between us that I couldn't quite put my finger on. Of course, I had no idea at the time that I was speaking to a woman who had prior convictions and who would later be arrested for child trafficking. The uneasiness I had felt, was my gut gently nudging me to see what was really happening behind the cartoon printed curtains in her derelict 'sanctuary' as she liked to call it.

Running an unregistered establishment for orphaned or abandoned children was her business and she defrauded charitable donors, which resulted in compounding the neglect that the children in her care had previously experienced.

Always trust your intuition. If you feel something is wrong then it is probably because it is.

Living with the Condom Boy and his younger brother, was a trio of sisters who were born one year apart and were all under the age of 11. What first struck me when I met them was that they were carbon copies of each other. Their deep blue eyes and their fair skin, framed by their blonde shoulder length hair, brought with them the label of pretty. Unlike the boys I was working with, they missed their mom and cried every night because they wanted to go back and live with her. I didn't know the history behind their situation, but when I was eventually asked to coach them, I had a sneaking suspicion that it would be trickier than working with the boys.

The sisters had heard from Condom boy how "nice" I was and it was their idea to ask for coaching. They initiated the conversation, and under the supervision of the corporate sponsor, I agreed to coach them. "Can we swim in your pool?", became the younger sister's mantra. "Take us home with you, so we can live in your big house," she used to chant. She spoke in such a determined little voice but it was each time dampened by her older sisters insistence that mom was coming to fetch them.

The irony of the matter was that as a childless mother of none, I so desperately wanted to take these girls home to live with me. I started day-dreaming of what it would be like to have our home filled with a gaggle of giggly girls. I spoke to nobody about my thoughts, but I started becoming closer to the girls as a result of my own inner need to be a mother. I was transferring my needs onto them and I can say with total conviction that this was one of the things that contributed to the mental breakdown I experienced that followed a few years after.

These girls had a story that no ears deserved to hear. Unlike the condom boy who sat with his brother outside his mom's flat waiting for her to finish her sex work, these girls told their own version of a happy story.

Of a mom who loved them and who fed them and who took them shopping and who read them stories at night. In their eyes, it wasn't their mom's fault that some of the men that she had called her boyfriends had molested them. These men were manipulative and had given them cheap gifts that they cashed in for a fondle.

The older sister claimed it was because they were pretty, whilst the middle sister insisted that they did it because they were lonely. The younger sister just said she liked the toys. It turns out that whilst the two younger sisters were only being molested, their pre-teen sister was being serially sexually abused with her mother's knowledge.

Being a needy woman, she relied on her good looks to lure men in that would 'pay' for her lifestyle. The trade-off was selling her daughter's virginity, just as I would later find out she had traded hers at the same age.

Embracing potential is more than just a temporary solution

The children in the shelter were tiny specks of dust in the greater scheme of humanity, yet their story mirrored those before and after them with such clarity, that I felt a sense of hopelessness that overwhelmed my professionalism. I became immersed in volunteering my coaching services to the children at the shelter, until the words of the little boy with the scar above his left eye became my wake-up call.

Through the endless beatings caused by his father's drunken rages, he spoke sense and he had the foresight to say it as it was. "You're going to leave like everybody else does." He was right, I was going to leave. I was going to carry on living my own life. I was unable to rescue them. He was so so right.

Isn't that like most of us who volunteer our time. We feel good at the time, but when the outreach is no longer sustainable, we carry on living our lives which appears as rejection to those left behind. True volunteers are those who are in it for the long haul. They stay and they serve and they commit their time and energy to bring about long-term changes. Unfortunately, in this context, I wasn't the latter.

At this stage, I knew my work had been done and whilst at face value, it appeared that I had coached the kids to embrace their potential, what had really happened was that I had been the healing balm under the temporary band aid that Social Services had given them in their derelict shelter whilst waiting for placements.

The last time I saw the pretty sisters was when I visited the orphanage where they had been temporarily housed. Their social worker told me it was highly unlikely they would be fostered or adopted together. I was horrified at this notion, but her prediction turned out to be true.

Awareness is all about transforming ignorance through truth

Condom Boy and his brother went to live with a seemingly respectable foster family and all that they left behind was the remnants of their story and the guilt that I had not done more.

How many well-intentioned adults like myself get wrapped up in doing what we think is good at the time and then realising that we have over committed and we can't properly follow through? The truth is that charity work, especially in the children's arena, is very much like this, with people losing the essence of the children and being more focused on ticking the boxes.

I certainly am not a box ticker, but at that stage I think I may have benefitted more than the shelter children that I worked with. They filled my gaping hole of not being a mom and I used them to ease my burden and shift my thoughts to something other than my own needs. I know that I left them with lessons of their own, but I do know that I gained more than they probably did.

Emotional freedom is about creating a space for reflection

My cousin, born just two weeks before me, incidentally also has a great love for children. He bravely shifted careers in his forties from working in decorating to becoming a care worker for a major childrens' charity in the UK. The experiences that he has shared with me have been eye opening. In such a large organisation, there are still people slipping through the cracks who don't have that secret core ingredient of passion for children.

Some of his colleagues see it as their job to placate an autistic child with harsh words, often lacking in the much needed compassion they deserve. This disturbs him as it does me. Luckily, he works alongside many carers who share his enthusiasm, but paperwork bogs them down, and the endless rules that negate the real needs of the children leave them feeling frustrated.

There is so much that can be done by adults in institutions to leave children coping better and feeling worthier. It all starts with education. Many fail to understand the psychology behind the premise that all "bad" behaviour in a child is simply a sign of an unmet need. It is us adults who seem to be missing the boat and not meeting those needs adequately. Children simply act out when they have no other forms of expression.

The impact of our words and our actions on a child's self-worth should never be under estimated. The teachers in Condom Boys school belittled him and had no insight into what he was really going through, and his story is not unique. I have seen this happen first hand in the schools I have taught in with children who are labelled as academically weak being made to feel they have failed when in fact it is the adults and the system that is failing them. So many children display emotional problems in the classroom that mimic Attention Deficit Hyperactivity Disorder (ADHD), and why educated teachers are still failing to see the connection I still cannot understand.

A child who is traumatised, neglected, abused or stressed will never perform well in a mainstream school setting. What they need first and foremost is a safe space to learn within their own parameters, on their own time, and in their own style. Unfortunately, this is seldom catered for in schools, and many children fall under the radar and learning difficulties perpetuate when they could easily have been avoided.

When I was a lecturer at a university for teaching students, I would go into my first lecture of the semester with these words: "You are not being trained to teach. You are being trained to motivate."

My students used to look at me with dumbstruck faces probably questioning the mental stability of this lecturer with odd ideas, however by the end of each semester, my students would get it. They understood the value of tapping into a child's potential and not measuring their worth according to a score on a report card.

My wish is that every university that grooms teachers to enter the classroom, finds it within themselves to add life coaching for children to the curriculum. So much can be done when adults themselves are better equipped.

The bitter taste of reality can be hard to swallow

Condom Boy and his brother and the 3 sisters have all left a gaping hole in my heart. What used to be there was my intact view of the world. That it is a good place. My first-hand exposure to their stories and how vulnerable they were gave me a taste of reality that I didn't want to deal with. I avoided the truth because it was hard for me to bear.

The truth was that I myself needed help because I had issues I needed to deal with and I was transferring my baggage into my coaching space. Unintentionally I was using my coaching as an escape from myself. I don't know if it was fair on the children but I can only hope that what I perceive as me letting them down on one level was, to them, rewarding on another. Since most of the adults in their life had let them down, I feel really uncomfortable thinking I may also have contributed to that.

Too many adults look the other way when they see what is happening in plain sight. Like the needy mother of the three sisters, who was too scared to speak the truth and choose her offspring over the men who were abusing them. She was insecure and probably a victim herself who longed for love but was looking for it in all the wrong places.

I do know that I did lots of good for the kids in the shelter, but I also now have no way of seeing how the seeds I have planted have grown. Such is life but my belief is that when you coach children, it should be a long-term commitment. You don't dip in and out as you see fit. It wasn't my choice to not continue coaching the children as they were put into foster care and orphanages, but ideally, I would have liked to have been that solid pillar of support that tracked their progress through the care system.

I wasn't able to do that not only because it was logistically impossible, but I think if I had continued, I may have come apart at the seams. I can only hope that they watered their own seeds I had planted, because most of the adults in their life certainly weren't doing it for them.

What I do know is this: It can take just one adult to change the trajectory of a child's life. For the positive or the negative. The choice is ours. Those children changed my life to one of heightened awareness and started the unravelling that would eventually lead me to my greatest personal growth. I am grateful for the lessons they shared with me.

The Hidden Truths about neglect:

- *Sometimes children's negative behaviour is tied to a complex web of reasons that evade your initial understanding. It is about peeling back the layers that hamper true potential.*

- *When it comes to children, choose to leave other people's negative perceptions at the door and form your own opinions based on having a genuine interest in who they really are.*

- *Your childhood does not define you, it is what you do with the lessons you learnt that does.*

- *Adults over commit all the time. When they let children down, it breeds distrust and plants the seeds for a bad relationship.*

- *Children act out when they know no alternative form of expression. Their behaviour is simply telling us a story that they cannot say in words.*

- *Motivating children to overcome their challenges is an ongoing process, not measured by time but by progress.*

- *Adults transfer the baggage of their own issues into children's lives with no malicious intent, but almost always with repercussions that could have been avoided.*

- *Too many adults have lost the essence of supporting children and are simply box tickers who have no empathy or foresight to do anything else.*

- *Failing to see the connection between emotional problems and academic problems is short sighted. A child cannot learn if they are in emotional overdrive.*

- *Sometimes we need to completely unravel in order to experience our greatest inner growth. It is okay to reinvent yourself.*

5

WHEN YOU ARE HUNGRY EAT CAKE

Hidden Truth:
Your childhood doesn't define you

He was handsome and strong, but weathered from living outdoors in the brash heat and contrasting cold during his childhood years. He towered over me with a glare in his eye stating the obvious, "You are white, I am black. You live in a mansion, I live on the street." With 7 more of 'him' walking through the door, I scrambled to respond.

"Yes, you are black and I am white but you are here and so am I. That is what we have in common." Open smirks and stifled laughs permeated my Kids Life Coaching space as one by one, the damaged and jaded youth flopped onto my strategically positioned bean bags. The room was filled with a stark animosity and what at the time I perceived to be contempt, because they were there through a charitable handout, not choice, and to me it felt obvious that they resented the fact.

I had been approached by a charity to work with these rehabilitated ex street children. They had spent their childhood living on the stark streets in the mild climate of my hometown Durban. They were hardened by their many days of begging and some of them stealing or sniffing glue. Their priority was survival, whilst mine at that stage was to give away my services for free in a bid to tame my conscience.

"So you think you can rescue us, white girl?" At the risk of sounding like a saviour out to conquer the world, I remember that as being my moment to prove my worth. How would I respond in such a way that it would make them trust me?
After what felt like ages, I finally spoke:

"As I said, you are here and so am I. You know where the door is so if you want to leave feel free. If you want to stay, then the rule is simply this. Remember Respect." Again, a few sniggers and I realised this was merely a tactic to gain ground and build a hierarchy. I didn't know it for sure then, but their perception was right. I was just a "white girl" living in a good neighbourhood in a big house, driving a nice car. I had been raised in a stable working class family but had never known hunger, nor felt the fear of not being supported by a parent.

Survival is about more than food and shelter. It is also about dignity and self-respect.

For these youth, their whole lives had been about survival and here I was, a white woman about to "show them everything would be okay." They were a tight knit group, almost like a little family, and they were proud of this, although their eyes betrayed their true feelings - a yearning to be valued and understood by those not in their inner circle.

They were hardened by life and as a consequence their coping mechanism was to put up a wall so high and so wide that nobody could possibly try to scale it and enter into their hearts and minds successfully. If you had to look at this behaviour in context, it was because as children, they had lived on the street and endured hardships cast upon them without their choice. Hardships that no child should ever endure.

Some had run away from home because of abject abuse, poverty and joblessness that led to their parents sending them to beg to put food on the table. Most, however, were there because their parents had succumbed to the fate of an illness which was related to a variety of causes, but commonly it was either their HIV diagnosis or Tuberculosis (the silent killer when infected with the virus). Either way, they were victims of circumstance who lacked in parental involvement and were left to fend for themselves in dangerous situations on the street 24/7.

At this stage I need to define that 'street children' is a term used to describe children experiencing poverty and homelessness that are insufficiently protected and who are living on the streets of a city, town, or village.

UNICEF (United Nations International Children's Emergency Fund), who empowered this widely used definition, was established in 1946 to meet the needs of post-war children in China and Europe. Currently they confirm that the exact number of street children displaced worldwide is impossible to quantify, but it is likely to number in the tens of millions or higher, and some estimates place the figure as high as 100 million.

In practice, every city in the world has some street children, including the biggest and richest cities of the industrialised world. Many are just blind to the fact simply because they choose not to see.

Having travelled extensively throughout Europe, Asia and Canada, and having lived in London, I can say with conviction that I have seen very few instances of street children in the larger cities I have visited. In fact I can't recall seeing any children homeless and on their own in London like is evident on the streets of my home country South Africa.

Sometimes we are blinded by beliefs that shape who we are but aren't necessarily true

I have yet to visit all parts of the world, so I can only comment from my own view, but I can't imagine a child on the streets of London or New York begging without social services intervening very quickly, or somebody standing in to aid them within a day or two.

Although there are lots of charities in South Africa who support Street Children, such as the one that approached me, it is not uncommon to drive past the same children day in and day out standing at the same traffic light begging. The infrastructure is just unable to carry the load and intervene in ways that make a lasting impact. Worse yet, is the complacency of adults who see these children as a hindrance and complain about their begging. They negligently voice their opinions, but with no substance and worse yet, with no action taken to change the situation.

This is proven in a debate that I was involved in that started on Facebook when somebody posted a photo of a black child no older than 12, sitting in the middle of a busy intersection in a coastal town of Kwa Zulu Natal, begging. The predominantly white adults were of the opinion that this child was a nuisance and was maliciously making a choice to sit there and cause the possibility of an accident. I told them in no uncertain terms that the child was a victim and it is the adults who had let him down. They just didn't get it.

Some of them were so thick skinned and so narrow minded and conditioned by racism that they honestly justified their responses by claiming that it was a safety issue. Did any of those people stop their car, get out and remove the child to safety? No. Did any of them report the child to the police or social services? No. So why then complain and make an issue of it if you aren't prepared to actually do something about it?

Never generalise your outlook because of past history

As an emerging market and one of the leading suppliers worldwide of natural resources, there are daunting economic and social problems in South Africa that have been inherited from the apartheid era. One of these is the abundance of homeless children begging their way to a full belly and to often fund the glue sniffing habit that eases their pain. Street children are highly visible, yet, paradoxically, they are also among the most 'invisible' and therefore the hardest children to reach with the vital services that they need such as education and health-care. Just like is illustrated in this Facebook debate. Everybody has opinions on what other people can do but nobody is prepared to do it themselves.

Other than on social media, when I was living in South Africa, I have witnessed many upper and middle income people blatantly treating these children as offensive in their begging and they avoid any contact with them, with some even dishing out verbal abuse as to the nuisance they cause. Some I have seen at times curry favour with their conscience and dole out a few coins to appease their guilt, but for the most part it is the large charitable Street Children's organisations such as the one I assisted that are doing the groundwork in salvaging these children's lives.

Many years ago, my husband and his friends stopped at a beachfront take away in Durban for a snack. While his friends were inside getting food, my husband was on his phone outside. He unwittingly became the target of a mugging. His muggers were all children below the age of 12. One had a knife to his throat while the others rummaged through his pockets to steal his wallet, take his watch, phone and even his Mont Blanc pen that couldn't possibly have had any value to them. He could have been bitter, like so many other South Africans, but I respect his dignity in seeing that these were simply kids lost to the system because of circumstances. Maybe it was his many years of listening to me go on about these children being victims, but it couldn't have been easy to have had his space invaded that way. I am sharing this because many like my husband have experienced the same, so I do understand why many people feel the way they do.

One of the things that still confuses my heart was when I was told stories by the ex-street children that many of them found it to be more favourable to live on the street and be with their friends than to live with their families. They believed they had a place of identity and belonging there and it felt like they were part of a "real" family.

Many street children live in 'pods' and what would traditionally be identified as a gang, but in their street terminology, they describe themselves as a family complete with a "father figure" leader who carefully shares the food and their earnings for the day. I think it is beautiful the way these children have adapted and learnt to share the only thing they have to give away to each other for free. They share their love to and for each other even though adults have put them in the position of having to fend for themselves.

A lesson in humility is valuable when it is received with grace

I still remember the feeling that first day when I heard one recognisable Zulu word "Haibo" from one of the young men in my studio. He was the same one that had challenged me about my wealth and being white, when he first walked in. He was wearing a red T-shirt peppered with tiny holes from years of wear and although he had been removed from the streets and had a place to live, and an internship albeit with a meagre income, he still had an unease about him. It was as if he was intimidated by my presence but at the same time he was confident enough to launch into a full length discussion with his peers in his language and I couldn't understand one word.

I am still embarrassed as a white South African to admit that I have never become fluent in the Zulu language which is native to Kwa Zulu Natal where I lived almost my entire life, yet my black counterparts who had lived on the street with no proper education, could speak English.

I did understand this particular word and it signalled a dismissive "no" but I did not understand the rest of the conversation which consisted of colourful hand gestures between each of the young adults sitting in my coaching space, their dark skins a strong contrast to my brightly coloured bean bags. The fact that I didn't understand Zulu, and so had to request a translation was yet another strike against me along with my middle income upbringing and my very white life that was abundantly privileged.

With a clear lead by the ex-Street Children, winning hands down in what I suppose to an outsider would have looked like a territorial and hostile take-over in my space, I was relieved when one of the pretty ladies who was impeccably dressed in a summer dress and matching sandals, commanded her peers to revert to my mother tongue. I remember trying to hide my sigh of relief, as I desperately abandoned my insecure thoughts that the foreign words of a language I should long ago have learnt were vindictive in nature.

Complacency is no excuse when you have had all the opportunity

At the time, the black children I had been coaching in my practice were mainly upper income children with parents who were well educated, and in professional jobs such as a Pediatrician and a radio DJ. This was new territory to me and I had no vantage point other than my heart that was full of initial sympathy yet a strong desire to convert my counterproductive emotion into empathy which would prove to be more relevant and empowering.

Incidentally, one of the first conversations I had with them went something like this: "I want you to know up front that I don't feel sorry for you, I don't pity you, I don't want to give you any favours, I am also not interested in your history. What I am interested in, is getting to know you as the amazing person you are in this moment. I want to encourage you and support you to find the life you so deserve."

Oh boy. How naive I was then. I remember being met with blank stares that shared the real truth that I didn't really get it. I did pity them and I did want to give them favours and I did want to know about their history. In fact, I was fascinated to learn from these resilient youth who had overcome the odds.

Empathy is more productive than sympathy

Early exposure to trauma and high levels of stress affect the developing brain, particularly in those areas involved in emotions and learning. In these youth, their brain architecture had been forever changed by their childhood. All children who enter into their adolescence with a history of adversity and lack the presence of a consistent, loving adult to help them through it, are susceptible to developing mood disorders and to having poor executive functioning and decision-making skills.

These youth were no different and their way of functioning was completely foreign to me as an ex school teacher. I had seen parental neglect in my years in the classroom and I had also taught children in the foster care system and in orphanages but those children were different. They were never left to fend for themselves on the streets. I cannot help but admire those youth for overcoming their trauma in the only way they knew how.

Unfortunately, their primary coping mechanism was to block out any perceived threats automatically, and this dramatically stunted their ability to learn and build relationships. This forced me to approach my coaching from a new angle that I had never explored before, one that opened my mind to the possibility that any person no matter their background can be coached to achieve their full potential.

All their lives, these brave souls had been frowned upon and disrespected. They were used to people who felt sorry for them, feeding them their leftovers and tossing them an occasional coin. I did not want to be one of those people although I was offering their coaching with no expectations in return.

Deep down I knew that I was guilty just like everybody else of over sympathising and under empathising. I just had no frame of reference to what it must have been like for them, just like they had no frame of reference as to what my life was like.

At the time, my biggest problem was trying to fall pregnant even though three fertility specialists had told me it wasn't going to happen easily. Back then, I was still convinced I would be a mom in the traditional sense.

Their biggest problem was mapping out their future, and I had been tasked to help them with that. How does one map out a future if your past doesn't allow you to? How do you break somebody from the strangle hold of their history so that they can become the fullest version of themselves?

I was well aware of the perception these youth must have had of me with my glistening diamond ring and neatly French manicured nails which were testament to the fact that I lived a pampered and highly enviable lifestyle in comparison to them. Living on the streets as kids had hardened them and robbed them of their dignity and self-respect and I more than anything wanted to support them to rebuild their lives using the building blocks in their mind.

Putting things into perspective is about looking at the world through fresh eyes

At first, they were empty and mostly devoid of love, but later. I saw a healthy yearning to be uplifted with the sincere encouragement that I gave them over the months I coached them. So, I did what I knew best. I gave them unconditional, unconventional, upbeat, upliftment. This is now part of my Coaching model that I teach to people around the world. It is so simple yet so impactful and it all started with these youth who showed me that sticking with tried and tested traditional methods would not work for them.

I adapted my coaching to suit their needs. I focused on their strengths, which at first were hard to identify, and I worked at minimising their weaknesses. I explored new ways of doing things, and tailor made my coaching programme to suit their needs, which were consequently many.

To this day I see this as one of my biggest but most rewarding learning curves because not only did they grow in confidence, but I grew in my humility. They taught me to take a step back and value the fact that I had been showered with opportunity because of my birth right into a white family.

A schooling curriculum in real life is what sets leaders apart

I felt humbled by the fact that although these young people had every reason to hate the world, they were fighters with a true resilient spirit and they still had a spark in them that refused to be put out. I felt guilty when I thought now of the many days in my youth when I had complained about too much homework at school or about the fact that I wasn't allowed to go to a party with my friends, or about eating my vegetables at the dinner table. Childhood problems that weren't real problems in the greater scheme of things.

There are so many children who are fussy eaters and complain about the food they are fed. They don't know real hunger like street children do. They feel entitled to have three choices of cereal for breakfast and being able to go to Mc Donald's for a burger after school.

I find it sad that many of the parents I have worked with feel the need to "cater" for their child's appetite by serving them only chicken nuggets because "that's all my child eats". This is created by adults. Full stop. End of story.

As a non-parent it is easy for me to stand on the outside and look in, but surely when there are hungry children starving in Africa, it is a parent's job to put things into perspective for their fussy eater child?

The same goes for having too many toys and wearing only the nicest brand labelled clothes. Where do kids learn about this? From the media, but most of all from parents. Neglect comes in various forms, and parents who serve their children's needs 24/7 and bow down in submission to avoid conflict, are doing just as much of an injustice as the parent who has sent their child to beg on the streets.

A sense of entitlement is what is breaking down our youth's ability to be empathetic and caring contributors to our world. These ex street children had no sense of entitlement. In fact, they were of the opinion that they owed the world something and not the other way around. A healthy way of thinking even if caused by their adversity.

Sometimes we don't realise how lucky we really are until we see how unlucky somebody else is

Whilst coaching this group of ex street kids, there was one particular young man who relayed to me the story of him being top of class at school. When he was 12 he was forced to drop out of school after his parents died in a tragic accident using the notoriously unsafe "taxi" system of transport reserved for black people.

He traded his school books for newspapers, that became the blanket that covered him at night but his thirst for learning never stopped. His aspiration was to become a lawyer and he was one of the young people who did show a significantly higher intelligence. Not only did he borrow many of my Psychology and Self Development books as his own self prescribed reading, he had insightful debates with me before and after our coaching sessions. He is testimony to the fact that attitude towards learning is based on mindset and that adversity can only knock those down who believe that it has the power to do so. Coaching is about planting seeds of hope and it was a pleasure to help him grow those seeds.

To put this in context, I need to share that my very elementary and conflicting research has highlighted that in the eighties, the Apartheid government of South Africa spent an average of three times more on education for each white child, than they did for every black child. The quality of teaching staff also differed and education opportunities were heavily skewed towards preferential treatment for whites. It was also common for black children to attend school for fewer years than white children and in the case of these ex-street children, this was no exception, with the average school drop-out rate being age 12.

The first time I saw a black face in my school was in my final year when I was 17 years old. I befriended her and remember my mom, who was a teacher at my school, being a great role model in this regard. She was isolated because of the colour of her skin, and at the time I was Head Girl of the school and so I assumed the role of hostess and did what I could to make her integration as the first person of colour into a school of previously all white girls smoother.

In fact, when I was learning to drive, she was unfortunate enough to be part of my first mini fender bender. My mom and I would drive her home since she lived close to us with her mom, who was a domestic worker and living in an outhouse, or "khaya" in the Zulu vernacular. I remember her being so quiet in the backseat as my mom moaned at me for not concentrating, and rightly so.

At the time I can only imagine she was wondering how she would ever learn to drive if her mom was earning below minimum wage cleaning her bosses' home.

Don't lay blame,
give the feeling a name

The first few weeks of coaching those youth went by in a whirlwind of the group liberally spreading their verbal abuse around, chastising each other, speaking with hatred and laying blame. Their English was good, but still stilted and full of street slang that I often didn't understand, making our communication challenging at times.

One hour was never enough because after the 'bucket sessions' as I called them, they left feeling agitated, tired and deflated. At the best of times, working with a group brought with it a tricky dynamic, but this was off the charts. Most weeks, there were two or more participants missing from our session, with no excuse ever offered. They had never had the luxury of explaining themselves to somebody who cared, and to top it all off, they didn't seem to care what I thought anyway. They didn't understand the protocols of working within a diary and that my time was valuable, as was theirs.

My frustration increased as I started running out of ideas to engage them fully. My toolbox was running low and I was becoming desperate for a solution. I decided we needed a change of scenery and that perhaps a little detour off the beaten track would do the trick. My spirit of 'Ubuntu' had kicked in and I was keen on not only introducing this resilient group to something that took them out of their comfort zone, but that would also teach them a valuable life lesson.

Ubuntu is an ancient African word meaning 'humanity to others'. It also means 'I am what I am because of who we all are'. This concept underpins the vision statement of my organisation, where the success of my network of Kids Life Coaches is dependent on the success of the children we coach. I was to use this as a catalyst for engagement.

The spirit of "Ubuntu" and togetherness is within all of us

The turning point for my frustrations came when, I announced with much pomp and ceremony at the end of our session, that I was going to take them for coffee. Again, blank stares that couldn't hide the fact that they had absolutely no idea what I was talking about.

"You mean you make coffee?". He was the brightest of the group, the self-appointed spokesperson, often translating misconstrued statements. "No," I replied, "we are going to go to a restaurant and a waitress is going to serve us coffee." Probably due to the fact that nobody had ever served them anything, they keenly observed me as I spoke. "So next week, let's have a bit of fun!"

When we arrived at the tiny independent coffee shop the following week, it was an experience that was fraught with positives and negatives. We were frowned upon, as the majority of the group arrived wearing clothes that although perfectly neat and clean, didn't quite meet the unwarranted and unwritten expectations of the establishment.

Most of the patrons of the restaurant, who were white, were clearly not happy, with some even staring us down and making muted insults under their breaths. It wasn't the first time that this had happened to these ex-street kids, so I am not sure if it bothered them. But it bothered me. A lot. I experienced first-hand what they were exposed to on a daily basis and I didn't like the feeling.

What I do remember, was the desperate tugging at ill worn T-shirts, as they were taken out of their comfort zone. Clothes are not a measure of a man, but they certainly do help to build confidence. I cannot help but question how things would have been different if I had bought them each a new shirt and shoes so that they "fitted" the desired unwritten dress code of the establishment.

I ordered a cappuccino for each of us and a variety of cake slices to share. Being accustomed to sharing food on the streets, this communal gathering became a revelry of fun, as we sipped and snacked together. Many comments were made on the taste sensations they experienced and they learnt the names of treats that many of us take for granted such as "Carrot Cake" and "Chocolate Ganache Cake" and "Lemon Meringue Pie".

Their daily staple diet was maize porridge with the occasional brisket for meat, and door stop sandwiches with little more than butter and processed polony on a good day.

Value yourself first and others will do the same to you in return

I cannot measure the success of my attempt to give them an experience out of the norm, but that day, the lesson that they took away with them was that they were deserving of respect. That life had plenty more to offer them than what the harsh and unforgiving streets had taught them.

After this, it seemed that I was redeemed and our group fell into a new routine. Each week, I would bring cake to their group coaching sessions and they would sample the flavours and sip on coffee. Attendance soared as a consequence and it was on this high with everybody present and on time for a change, that we addressed a beyond sad situation a few weeks later.

One of the youths, who had suffered intermittently from substance abuse, had succumbed to the lure of his addiction and died of an overdose. I was devastated and visibly shaken, but realised now more than ever, the challenges that these young people were facing, with the odds always stacked against them.

Little did I know that this death would not be in vain and it served as an incentive for the other youth to focus their attention not only on staying alive, but also on finding their own happiness.

The young man who never spoke because of his poor command of English and who always sat quietly, observing, had simply broken the news to me with two words when I questioned why his friend wasn't there, "He's dead."

There appeared to be no compassion but I know deep down there was. These young people just didn't know how to express their feelings like I did. I felt sad, and the tears streaming from my eyes were hopefully one of their biggest lessons I gave them. I would like to think that they realised then that all feelings are okay and that sharing them is a way to lift our burden.

They didn't cry with me, but at least they knew I cared. I can only hope that our unspoken agreement that day where they allowed me to grieve, showed them that it was okay to show your grief even when nobody else does.

The truth is that the odds to stay alive in that room were questionable because the reality was that HIV/Tuberculosis, STD's were lying in wait for most of them like the grim reaper. They knew death well and it was a norm for them. It wasn't for me, so I struggled with the concept of possibly losing more members of my tight knit group.

Sadness is not always reflected through the tears we cry

With the months flying by, I started doubting my effectiveness as a coach less and less and the initial immense guilt at being white and privileged subsided. I knew that therapy was potentially on the cards for some of these youth who had the possibility of becoming very troubled adults. No amount of coaching would change their deeply ingrained hurt nor take away the memories of neglect and abuse. However, what I did manage to do was change their belief systems.

With persistence, I penetrated their tightly meshed resolve that initially wouldn't allow me in. They learnt to value themselves as humans first and that inner perception began to reflect on their outer world as others began to notice. The real turning point however came when I decided to tell them my truth about why I had originally decided to take them on as a pro bono case.

"I believe in you with all of my heart and I dream of the day that you can hold your head up high. I have grown to love you and yes, I do at times still feel sorry for you, but perhaps this is the problem. Feeling sorry for you has made me start feeling sorry for myself again. I am a mother of many, but I can't be mother of one. I feel anger towards your parents even though I have not met them because they abused or abandoned you, even though I don't know the real story. I can't have children of my own, because God has other plans for me, and seeing you like this, helpless, has left me feeling helpless. I judge your parents for letting you down. I would have given anything to be your parent."

The message underlying my tribute was that I was guilty of feeling sorry for myself and that I was full of anger at the injustices that I was facing because I couldn't have a baby. I gave them a mouthful of rambling words that I thought might be meaningless to them, but then to my surprise, I saw a ripple effect of affirmative nods. Had they understood, or were they just acknowledging me out of the respect and trust that I had earned?

What happened next, I did not anticipate, but one of the youths got up and walked across the room to me. She threw her arms around my neck. She hugged me tight and wouldn't let go. There was a hushed silence in my coaching space as one by one, they took turns hugging me. This was a major breakthrough not only for me, but for them, because it is only when we begin to love ourselves that we can begin to love others.

I am still in contact with a few of these beautiful souls, who have become parents, are successfully employed and living an honest and decent life in their own home, with a mobile phone, nice clothes and food on the table. They are testimony to the power of the human mind and how unconditional love and support can ultimately conquer all.

The Hidden Truths behind discrimination:

- *Never underestimate the power of your intentions. When you decide to make a positive impact in somebody's life, you will.*

- *Feeling sorry for somebody is disempowering and self-serving. It is often coupled with guilt because you feel helpless for not being able to do more.*

- *Having empathy is not about putting yourself in somebody else's shoes momentarily. It is about walking the road with them in ill-fitting shoes that hurt you just as much as they hurt the person you are walking beside.*

- *Resilience is the one good thing born out of neglect. Many children who have been abused as children have gone on to achieve great things as adults.*

- *It is only when we choose to be vulnerable and speak our own truth that we can truly connect with the human spirit.*

- *Unconventional ways of doing things often trumps tried and tested techniques. What is written in text books is not always what works in real life.*

- *Giving unconditional love is the antidote to melting a stone heart. Love without expectations of anything in return will soften even the hardest of spirits.*

- *When you feel like a victim because an injustice has been done to you, always remind yourself that there is somebody else somewhere experiencing worse.*

- *Perspective is hard when you have been conditioned to think in a certain way. Breaking from the shackles of your past is about acknowledging past negative seeds planted in your mind.*

- *A child making choices based on survival often does a better job at problem solving than a child making choices who has been over indulged and feels entitled to help.*

- ·

6

THE PAIN BEHIND THE VEIL

Hidden Truth:
Culture can sometimes limit true potential

The first time she lifted her protective black 'shield' that covered her face, I was struck by the flawless beauty that distracted me from her sad eyes. As a mother of two active little boys below the age of 8, this Muslim mum looked uncharacteristically radiant, the polar opposite of most of the frazzled moms I saw in my coaching practice.

Although most people say the eyes are the window to the soul, her face that was usually hidden behind her niqab had a story that I would later on in our relationship, become very familiar with. I believe that her face was her biggest asset because it housed her brilliant mind, so it was an irony that this was the part that she hid from the world because of her choice of religion.

A niqab is a veil worn along with a head scarf that conceals the face of women in Islamic societies, leaving only their eyes exposed. It is mostly worn when a woman leaves her home and she is compelled to wear it until she returns. Some Muslim women wear coverings as a sign of modesty and a symbol of religious faith. This lady with the petite body and proud poise revealed a side of herself to me that showed both of these to a degree but she found wearing the veil to be invasive and forced upon her.

A veil worn in any form should be a personal and independent choice, free of social pressure, and some of the time it is, but in her case, it was forced upon her by her husband and parents. This was unlike many of her Muslim sisters who willingly accepted covering their face as a sign of their dedication to their spirituality.

In recent years, with the spate of Islamic terrorist attacks aimed at Westerners around the world, it has been called a security risk and a "flag of fundamentalism" and there have been calls to ban it. It is shocking to comprehend just how many terror attacks there have been in the West in modern times with our most prominent and hard hitting being the 9/11 attacks in 2001.

I, however, don't think that face veils are the cause behind this and can't see the relevance. Fundamentalism is the fungus rotting away at the core of a religion that is the home of many upstanding people who don't hold these radical views. With the media sensationalising this, most people have become intolerant of Islam and have a narrow view on it because they view it as a religion with women having a backseat which isn't always necessarily true.

This lady, that I will call Veiled Beauty, showed me her true feelings about her being stripped of her freedom. She expressed how trapped she felt behind a veil and her stark black clothes, week after week over the time that I knew her. She had true dedication and adoration for her religion, but this did not transfer to her husband who had been part of her arranged marriage. Plainly put, she made him sound like a monster and I can only assume that had I ever met him, I wouldn't have been able to acknowledge him with my trademark smile.

Behind every veil there are secrets that want to be whispered out loud

I knew too much about who he really was, all because his wife had chosen me to be her confidante through a tumultuous time where she felt completely alone with no one else to turn to. Although judgement can lead you to the risk of misplaced notions, I couldn't help but feel an aversion to his outlook and the way he suppressed his wife in a marriage that had been forced on her.

Not only did he force her to participate in his sexual fetishes against her will, but his favourite sport was to engage in domestic abuse for the most minor of things. His biggest abuse, she candidly claimed, was that he made a habit of humiliating her in front of her children. He called her names and belittled her position by undermining any discipline she tried to exert over the boys. This made her feel helpless and very resentful. This trickled over into her deliberately choosing to irritate her husband. She knew that whether she was passive or pushing his buttons, she would be the brunt of his rants that she was useless. So she made it a game which implicated herself as the guilty party in the declining behaviour in her sons, even though she was the victim.

Mothers, especially those of boys, are known to be fiercely protective even to the extent of protecting them when they do wrong. The psychology of the mother-son relationship has been studied and discussed throughout history since around 440B.C when Sophocles wrote about Oedipus Rex, a man who killed his father and slept with his mother.

Whilst this is extreme, this has become famously known as the Oedipus complex, which is a term that was used by Sigmund Freud in his theory of psychosexual stages of development. He used it to describe a boy's feelings of desire for his mother, and jealousy and anger toward his father where essentially, a boy views his father as a rival for her attentions and affections. Even though this theory is extreme, I cannot help but reference it because in the case of these two boys, there was evidence to me that their desire was not towards lavishing their mother with their doting attention, but it was to continue the terror regime their father had modelled to them.

Attachment theory is a concept in developmental psychology that states that children who have a strong attachment to their parents, have been given the stability and security which is the safety net they need to grow their personality.

Religious extremism
can cut the ties of rationality

In the case of these boys, they were emotionally stunted because they were bobbing out at sea without a secure attachment to either of their parents. Children who are rejected or who receive care and comfort inconsistently, tend to develop behavioural problems. These two were no exception, and although their mother knew that her tenderness and sensitivity would lead to their richer and more rewarding emotional life, she had isolated her heart as a means of self-preservation.

Nurturing mothers can help their sons develop emotional intelligence, encouraging them to talk about their feelings and recognise those of others. The irony is that had Veiled Beauty made an investment in her boys she would have ensured they would one day make strong, empathetic spouses, where their marriage would be based on communication skills and teamwork rather than brute physical strength, humiliation or dominance.

Arranged marriages are the cultural norm for some conservative Muslims across the world and both men and women who are ready to get married may meet their future spouse through family arrangements. Generally they don't *'date'* in the popular Western cultural sense, but the expectation is always there that the seed for love is planted and will continue to bloom after the marriage.

Usually before any candidates are considered, families as a unit decide the values and characteristics that potential spouses should have so the couple have a satisfying life together. At this point I wish to clarify that of the majority of the Muslim women I have spoken to, who have acquired their husbands through an arranged marriage, claim to be happy and fulfilled.

True love is found in expressing the freedom of your heart

Veiled Beauty was fortunate to have been chosen to enter into a family with a good name and lots of money, but she affirmed that this was not enough because what she really wanted was the freedom to be her own person. The shackles her family tied to her for a lifetime was a living nightmare that none of them were witness to because all they had seen was the fact that she was marrying into financial abundance and a life of endless luxury. This turned out to be her buffer for the pain, but it didn't substitute her true need for genuine affection, love and honour, which were traceless in her marriage.

After her initial introduction to her then future husband she was lucky enough to be granted the opportunity to meet with him in private, but under close supervision from female family members. Initially she had felt taken by his good looks, charm, and what she thought then was tenderness, but in the end just turned out to be the start of his manipulative tactics that would crumble her belief in his facade.

Although they had met prior to their wedding unlike some forced marriages where man and woman are united without their consent, she didn't really have a say in her fate. After her first meeting with him, she told her parents that she was not sure that she wanted to marry him and they reverted to the tactics of not speaking to her for days on end which she felt was akin to cutting the ties of the womb.

Their clear disapproval at her insolence for not wanting to be shackled to a man she may not love, was their threat to disown her from her own family who was financially held in high esteem and carried with them an elevated status. She had been brainwashed from a very young age to obey her parents' wishes to enter into an arranged marriage and her resistance was not something they had planned for.

Veiled Beauty's mom's marriage had worked, so why shouldn't hers? The difference was that she had chosen to educate herself and did not live in a Muslim country where there was no Western influence. She yearned for respect and needed to have her voice heard and her face seen, and her family were doing their utmost best to stifle her, which led to resentment that ate away at her happiness. She once said: "Food that one is forced to eat is unpleasant for a short while, but the bitter taste of a forced marriage lasts for a lifetime."

Drop the formalities if you aim to build a bond that transcends boundaries

In all of our interactions, I never did get to know her first name and through our written correspondence, I had come to realise that her title was merely that of her husband, with a Mrs tacked on the front. Although she was probably a similar age to me, she expected me to formally acknowledge her by her married name as if she was years my senior and was garnering my superficial respect.

Her husband was a prominent business man and if one had to class him, it would be as shrewd and street smart with a network of followers. She sported a sleek black Mercedes Benz with matching black leather seats which was like a matching accessory to her full black head cover and long black dress. The chauffeur that was employed to drive her and the boys around was tall and ruggedly handsome, and although he didn't wear what many perceive to be the chauffeurs outfit complete with gloves and cap, he was always impeccably dressed and a true gentleman opening and closing the door behind her. This she told me was one of the most respectful men in her life but she knew it was that way because her husband was responsible for feeding his entire family and so he was in essence paid to be polite.

Goodness comes from within and is reflected in how we treat strangers when nobody is watching

Initially, in our meetings, she avoided all eye contact, even when her boys addressed her. "Mammu, mammu," both boys whined incessantly whenever mom and I spoke. The thing that most surprised me, was that she did nothing to stop them. She just continued speaking to me as if her ears were gilded with metal, making her immune to their rudeness. Mine on the other hand were not, and these two were beyond what would commonly be perceived and classified as naughty.

I have always addressed bad behaviour as an unmet need, and in this case, I am grateful that mom had the foresight to seek me out and let her boys participate in my coaching sessions before their behaviour spiralled beyond easy intervention and repair.

She had identified that something was seriously amiss in her boys, and she instinctually knew that her erratic parenting had set her up for failure. She felt like a newly trained puppy doing tricks and learning as she went along and readjusting according to input from her sons.

Like their father, they manipulated her and coerced her into getting their own way and one of the defining moments where she finally knew she had to seek help was when they attacked her at dinner throwing their food in her face because she would not let them let them eat in front of the television. At the time, their father had been away on yet another extended business trip but had he been there, she was of the belief that he probably wouldn't have supported her in their disciplining anyway.

These boys who were privileged, well dressed and went to what was considered an elite school eventually came to rely on my objectivity that saw me standing on the fence that divided them from their mom and helping them to climb over to reunite with the love they secretly yearned for.

Children become what we make them and do what we teach them

The original query that I had received from her was for me to coach her two boys together, because as siblings they were constantly bickering. I initially assumed that this was a healthy dose of sibling rivalry, when in fact it was confirmed after meeting them that the two boys themselves were not each other's rivals, but their mom was actually at the mercy of their solidarity as brothers.

This was a clue that mom was needing me to take the lead since she seemed accustomed to this from her two boys. I perceived that culturally, she had been swayed into submissiveness, and that wearing a permanent shield on her face when entering the public domain was the reason for her lack of assertiveness. However I have to consider the fact that she behaved the same as any abused woman would no matter their culture or religion. I don't know the true reason, but the fact was that her children disrespected her and this was more than just a reflection of how they saw their father treating her.

I heard from her that their sibling rivalry turned out to be over petty things such as who got to operate the TV remote but this was soon settled when each boy was rewarded with their own television for their bedroom. Or the time when they argued in a restaurant because the one brother perceived his chocolate milkshake to have less chocolate and in protest upended the liquid over his brother's head. This was merely an extension of the previous 'food in the face' behaviour with mom that went unsanctioned and was rewarded with her silence rather than the consequences which would have prevented it from happening a second time around.

Look beyond the initial story
if you want to find the real answer

Little is known about the influences of religious beliefs and practices on raising children in the Muslim faith. Yet religious beliefs and practices have the potential to profoundly influence many aspects of life, including approaches to parenting. No matter the faith or religion, parents hold enormous leverage in terms of what they teach their children and accordingly how their children grow up into adults.

Islam holds parents accountable as to how they conduct their children's upbringing according to the guidelines of the Quran. This is not unique to this religion, because many households use their religious text to steer the direction of their family based on a foundation of key values.

The common ones shared by most religions include: speaking the truth, showing kindness and generosity, doing no harm to others and practicing forgiveness. The one, however, that is also common but that I certainly did not see displayed with the children of Veiled Beauty, was to show respect to your father and mother.

Perhaps in their home, the boys behaved differently towards their mother, but I can only assume that if they were so disrespectful to her in my presence then this must have been exponentially worse behind closed doors. It is unfair to assume that they were following the lead of their father, but over my many years of coaching children across multiple religious profiles, I can't help but deduce that Muslim boys in particular are the most rambunctious. Once again this is merely my observation and my own version of the truth.

My opinion has been derived from my experiences through teaching and coaching many such Muslim boys. I conclude it may well be because gender roles manifest themselves because men and women are allotted different rights and different cultural expectations. The truth was that for these boys, respect was a word foreign to them and this not only included for others and their possessions but sadly they had no respect for themselves either. This was one of the very pertinent issues I would tackle as their Kids Life Coach.

Staring the boys down was something I hadn't anticipated doing week after week, because nothing else seemed to show effect quite like that did. Initially upon entering my coaching space, they always started by babbling and spluttering and whining complaints at their mom. "It's too hot in here. I want to go home and watch TV." And so they went on and on and on.

They displayed a true malaise of modern Western culture with technology at the centre of these children's entertainment platform. This was a sharp contrast to the conservative notion of mom wearing her traditional religious covering in a democratic environment where liberalism and freedom of expression were supposedly upheld.

When I asked them to wait their turn to speak, they ignored me. When I explained the reason why they should wait their turn to speak, they ignored me. When I tried to reason that everybody would benefit, they ignored me. I saw a small glimpse of what mom must have felt like living with those two boys. With not a blink of an eye, they simply continued behaving in the way that they had been accustomed to for so long.

Rewiring their brains and getting them to flex their empathy muscles was somewhat more challenging than many other children I had worked with, but I did eventually see the results. The turning point was when I asked them in a coaching session to put on their mom's niqab, which she always removed when she was with me. This was rather controversial, but fascinated them, and the notion seemed incomprehensible. Yet when they had a small glimpse of life from behind the screen that blocked their mom's face from public view, there was a small shift in their understanding.

Family bonds are forged through genuine uninterrupted interaction that transcends daily routine

In a family coaching programme that I offer my clients, where the outcome is to forge family bonds and understand roles and responsibilities, one of the activities is for parents and their children to swop their shoes. The aim of this activity is for them to behave like each other at their worst and at their best for a few minutes with the outcome of understanding their behaviour better.

Although the way I had approached this with using the head instead of the feet would have been considered very controversial to some religious fanatics, that day the boys did get to "walk in their mom's shoes". To empathise with someone is to understand what they are feeling or, more properly, to understand how you would feel if you were in that situation.

This is an extension of self-concept, but it requires an awareness that others think of themselves in ways that are both similar to and different from the way you do, and that they also have emotions they associate with those thoughts and images.

Although the best training for empathy starts in infancy, these boys had a valuable lesson imprinted on them the day they saw the world from behind their mothers Niqab . At this stage I also want to share that I didn't in any way adjust my coaching methods that I used with these Muslim boys just because they were part of a different culture and religion. Over the years, my biggest strength in working with children has been in maintaining the integrity of my coaching model which does not deviate from the neutrality of respecting all children from all backgrounds, religions, cultures and circumstances.

Strength is sometimes hidden in places where we fail to look

Although your perception by now may be that mom was an insipid woman who held no strength in her own right, she turned out to be an intelligent lady, and initially I would coach her sons, feeding them with the skills to show more self- control and to make choices based on a respect for themselves and others. They were making good progress, but as the weeks passed, mom and I started spending more time conversing with each other about topics related not only to her sons, but to the world. When their coaching programme with me ended, and I was happy with the level of success that the boys had achieved, mom still insisted on continuing to pay me with her wad of crisp notes week after week, saying that she had begun to rely on my support.

Her sons, who after a few months of my coaching were calmer, more respectful and more content, played in my Kids Life

Studio reception area while we spent time unpacking the blackness in her mind. To this day I still acknowledge that she gave me the wonderful gift of inspiring me to develop my parent coaching programme.

Destiny unfolds in the most unexpected places when we just trust the process

Unlike other traditional parent interventions, this does not focus on child orientated outcomes, but looks at the parent enhancing their own self-awareness and working on the areas in their lives lacking in personal fulfilment. In a nutshell, I was coaching this mom to find her inner strength again and I was her cheerleader in the process. The fact that I wasn't a mother myself also brought with it the much needed neutrality and objectivity which didn't cloud my approach.

We had lengthy intellectual conversations where she disclosed the pain that I had seen hidden in her eyes from the first day we met. The most revealing of conversations was when she said, "They treat me with complete disregard, just like their father." I knew that the statement was loaded and was a silent plea for being treated with the respect she so deserved.

Being the only woman in her home meant a constant barrage of demands and expectations. Although she had a troop of servants cooking, cleaning and taking care of the boys' general well-being, she felt overwhelmed and utilised her time at home, behind closed doors, reading and writing.

Veiled Beauty's one true love affair that she refused to compromise on was with books, and she found comfort and possibility in the pages of the varied and complex titles she delved into. We had lengthy conversations about George Orwell's Animal Farm, the justice behind To Kill a Mocking Bird and poetry that spoke of both love and war.

We shared our dreams of becoming authors and sharing our stories with the world. She had a very valuable story to tell and she believed that she would die with it inside her, so she told me her story instead.

She secretly indulged herself in crafting her own book and she would bring me her work of art weekly to proof read for her.

Her writing was brilliant, with such eloquent prose, and the plot, which I had already had an insider's glimpse of, held me on the edge of my seat. The characters she had crafted were a mirror image of her life yet paradoxically a strong contrast to the reality she faced.

"This is great stuff!", was my initial reaction when she shared her guilty pleasure with me. I have a snapshot in my mind of her pride, not the kind that is arrogant, but the kind that says, "*I'll show you what I'm capable of, world*". Her ties to her husband and the role she had been cast in as subservient wife may have never allowed her to publish but what she was in fact doing was channeling her deepest desires into the pages of a book where she was unjudged and unashamed.

Dreams take flight in the imagination first

Although this one chapter in this book is dedicated to her, it by no means gives her life the dignity it deserves. I do secretly hope that she has adorned her beautifully crafted life in the pages of her own book that may share the shelves with mine under a pseudonym or, better yet, with her full faced portrait emblazoning the cover.

We have since lost contact, so if Veiled Beauty ever reads this, I hope that she knows that the impact she made on my life was immeasurable. She gave me more gratitude for the life of freedom I live, where the lipstick I wear and the earrings I don are visible to the world. Where I can appear in whatever colour clothing I want to and go wherever I want to go. Where I can show my knees and shoulders in public without scorn.

Most of all, I am forever reminded when I bicker at my husband for not taking out the rubbish, that this is small and insignificant in the greater scheme of things. I got to choose my own husband and we got to court each other without pressure or fear and for that I am grateful. Being a woman in this world is a lot more liberal than generations ago, but never be naive in the fact that some women are still enslaved as defined by modern democracies in situations beyond their control.

The Hidden Truths about culture and religion:

- *Religion can either join us in harmony or cause disunity. Extremism is the fatal attraction that has divided many nations.*

- *Dignity is something we feel when others treat us with respect. This is often lost because of an inflated sense of self-importance.*

- *Some men feel superior to women because they believe their religious text says so. Often their behaviour behind closed doors doesn't match the core of what this really means.*

- *Children who see their father treating their mother with disrespect will do the same. There is a risk of them turning out the same way when they one day become a spouse.*

- *The eyes are the window of the soul, and without freedom, they weep silent tears of regret.*

- *Anybody who is forced against their will into something will at some stage feel resentment.*

- *When somebody has nothing else to lose because no matter what they do, they will be judged anyway, they start living up to those expectations.*

- *Playing the game of dominance is like a drug to many men, who find a thrill in being the bread winner of the family, yet provide little emotional support.*

- *Money is merely a vehicle to more freedom. This freedom means nothing if you don't have respect from those that give it to you.*

- *Everybody has a gift inside of them planted there by God and all they need is somebody neutral to be the catalyst in helping them express that to the world.*

7

THE CIRCUS RING MASTER

Hidden Truth:
Death is inevitable, how we live is optional

She had been ill for a long time, the cancer eating away at her breasts and spreading rapidly into the rest of her body. The treatments were in vein and although she knew her prognosis was terminal, she remained positive and strong. An amazing woman that was always immaculately dressed and well- groomed when she dropped her two gorgeous girls off for their coaching sessions with me. Her instruction was brief and to the point at our initial consultation "Please can you prepare my girls for my death."

I was stunned as she explained all they had gone through over the 3 years prior that she had been ill. She described them as two beautiful girls, with an inner strength that she said was a true gift from God. They knew their mom wasn't well, but what they didn't know is that the doctors' had given her no more than 3 months before she succumbed to the untimely death that would leave them behind. She was preparing them for this eventuality and although her body was withering away her mind was fully able to plan a streamlined outcome for her girls.

"I have terminal cancer and I want my girls to be strong when I am gone. I have dreams for them and they are destined for greatness." I was in awe of her composure that did not betray her pain nor her fear. At that stage, I had no understanding of what my coaching would entail and I felt it fit to tell her this up front.

"I have no experience in terminal illness and death. As much as I would like to honour your request, it is only responsible of me to recommend an excellent trauma counsellor to you."

She held her stare and pronounced the words slowly, obviously in an attempt to make me understand. "Do you think I haven't tried that? We have been to a variety of psychologists, therapists and a pretty damn good trauma counsellor, but none of them are good enough for my girls."

My mind was whirling as I began to piece the puzzle together. Was it preventative skills training and ongoing motivation and support that was needed for her girls? I was confused as to what she actually wanted me to do?

Although I was well respected in the coaching field, I doubted my ability to surpass the expertise of medical professionals who were trained for situations like this. I had often worked with a variety of kids who had been through a long list of therapists, and were sent to me as a last resort, and I can say that that my success rate was 100% when all other resources were already exhausted. I didn't want to set myself up for failure and disappoint this determined lady but most of all, I didn't feel it fair to let her girls down.

Traditional text book methods aren't always the answer

I was once attacked on the professional social media network Linkedin for writing a controversial article on why I love being a child life coach as opposed to a child psychologist. It brought me lots of bitter words from the medical fraternity who took personal insult to my views. They had studied for years to over analyse peoples brains and I was publicly proclaiming that I did all the fun stuff and "played for a living".

Many ex-therapy clients saw quick results with me that they didn't manage to achieve in years with their psychologist. I believe this was simply because of my ability to tap into a child's potential through their language which is play.

I remember one particular psychologist who told me I was delusional to think coaching could make a difference to children. Yes maybe? However it depends on the precise definition. You see if delusional means getting the best out of children by equipping them with practical skills rather than reminding them of their pain...then I suppose I am.

Any good psychologist - and I have worked with many - understands the value of coaching children when done properly. It is only those who feel threatened by a new school of thought and a fresh way of doing things that will sling unfounded statements such as these.

I am like an ostrich. I bury my head in the sand and avoid speaking about or acknowledging pain especially when it comes to children. This same psychologist was of the opinion that the only reason I achieved success in the children who had abandoned therapy was because they had already done the groundwork for me.

The thing is that this confrontation in a public space, only served to cement my view that although therapy is necessary, in some instances, the very person delivering the service needs to change their outdated perception of the world, that is often confined to the pages of a textbook.

In my experience, sometimes it takes a multi-disciplinary team to support children. I am pleased that Kids Life Coaching is now being recognised as a respected member of that team and although being the ugly sister isn't always fun, I have earned respect through the value I provide. My success is dependent on the success of the children that I coach and their positive results have given me the momentum to lay the foundation for raising the standards of coaching children around the world.

So when the dying mom requested that I support her girls after stating her abandoned hope in what therapy offered, I knew in my heart that I wouldn't decline. I did what every responsible coach should always do though. I conditionally agreed. This was merely my safety blanket, but I knew I was going to work with these girls.

"Let me meet your girls first, before I commit to anything." was an answer that forced a smile onto her face and she dropped her shoulders, relaxing for the first time during our initial conversation.

"You will just love them." and off she went, explaining at length the girls and their unique character traits, their quirks, personality, strengths and talents. If anything, I was well prepared to meet the two of them or so I thought.

Never assume you know something until you dig for the hidden truth

Before meeting any child for an initial consultation, I always ask parents to complete a comprehensive online lifestyle assessment on my website, that focuses on key areas of their child's life. It helps me to get a snapshot of where that child may be out of balance and I use it as a blueprint for setting goals and tailor making their coaching plan.

According to their assessments, their mom was doing a great job on their lifestyle and according to her input the fundamentals were in place such as eating, sleeping, exercise and family time. I couldn't visibly see any red flags and usually this would mean that my coaching programme would be preventative in nature.

The reason for mom approaching me, did not reflect accurately on the assessment and it only showed up on one section which is 'stress relating to life'. This is the final section of my assessment where I look at environmental stressors and if these are impacting on a child's behaviour. Their stress was off the charts, but yet every other area including school and friendships was neatly proportioned as if they were just normal girls facing normal everyday challenges.

Although I was filled with trepidation, I remember looking forward to meeting the girls and when they arrived in my coaching space, for their initial family consultation, I was met with wide smiles. What surfaced during that exploratory session, was not only surprising, but also a bit concerning.

Mom was the 'elephant sitting in the room' and I was the Circus Ring Master. The girls were the tight rope walkers visibly teetering on the edge and with no safety net in place. The youngest was born from a different dad and not only looked different, but acted remarkably different to her teenage sister, and from the outset, I could see that they were two polar opposites. I knew instinctively that I wouldn't be able to coach them together as siblings like mom had requested.

I so desperately wanted to ask the question that I always ask my new clients "Do you know why you are here today?" but I knew this was something I was to avoid in this particular conversation.

A non-negotiable policy which I had never waived before, was that the kids that I coach had to choose to attend my programme. I did not allow parents to force or coerce their children to see me because, not only was there a stigma attached to the fact that there may be something "wrong" with them, but there was a strong possibility that they would be set up for failure if their free will was removed.

Always trust your instinct

Majority of my coaching success is about getting buy-in and at that stage, the girls were not forthcoming in that arena! They were digging their heels in with a kind of resistance that was tantamount to being downright rude. Not with me. Not with mom. But with each other. There was a blatant sibling rivalry evident that surpassed the norm.

Sibling rivalry is a common issue faced by most families, and it has been around as long as there have been brothers and sisters. It is that silent unspoken competition between siblings for the love, affection, and attention of one or both parents. Often vying for this attention is simply for recognition and a sense of acknowledgement. As close as siblings can be, they can also be fierce enemies and in the case of these girls there was a resistant tug to find the careful balance of their mothers attention.

One of the most common causes of sibling rivalry tends to be jealousy when a child may feel that they are not getting equal amounts of parental attention. While it is often true that a parent may be in some ways closer to one of their children than another, in this instance, I couldn't tell who mom preferred, or if indeed this was actually the case. She visibly worked hard to ensure that both of her girls felt loved, and got the attention that they needed.

"It's not fair!" the gorgeous brown eyed, olive skinned girl exclaimed. "She is older than me and always tells me what to do. It's just not fair!" As I stared into her eyes, I could see the tears welling up, and I knew that the real reason she was upset, was not because of her 'bossy' sister. It was because I think she instinctively knew that her sister would soon replace her mother in caring for her. As much as mom believed that her girls didn't know about her impending death, their intuition was razor sharp and their hearts were fracturing at a steady rate.

Speak about the hard things before it is too late and somebody else gets it wrong

I once had one of my certified Kids Life Coaches ask a question on our online forum about a mother she was dealing with. Her client's husband had died years prior and she had never found the right time to tell her child who had been a toddler at the time. Her child just came to believe that daddy was away for work.

This is obviously an extreme example, but hiding the truth from children can often do more damage than causing them the initial hurt. Sadness is a human emotion and although this mom was well intentioned because she thought she was protecting her child, can you imagine what will happen when the truth eventually emerges. Not only is she suppressing her own right to grieve the death of her husband, but she is wearing a mask that will forever separate her child from her in later years. That kind of act although coming from a place of preservation will do unspeakable harm to the underlying trust that should always be the basis of every parent child relationship.

"I understand that you don't think its fair, but let's make a list of the good things that your sister does for you." She stared at me defiantly "Well, I don't want to!" Usually the attitude of the youngest child in the family, plays into their sense of entitlement and this coupled with the stress, heartache and fear, had brought out a subtle yet determined rebellion in this little girl.

It turns out that this was not isolated to my studio, but was a daily occurrence in her home, where she made everybody walk on egg shells. Her mom was dying and somehow she knew it even though nobody had whispered the secret out loud. How on earth was I to comfort this girl and prepare her for the harsh blow life was due to give her. She was already grieving and I wasn't equipped to help. Well not in the traditional sense anyway.

Contrary to her younger sisters judgment that she was bossy, the young lady with the serene smile and the Bohemian wardrobe had a sense of peace and calmness about her. She appeared to have it together, but I knew the signs that proved otherwise. She was withdrawn and I was told she was losing weight at a steady rate. She avoided all human contact including her mom and substantiated this by saying that she loved being in her own company, feeding her dream of being a famous clothing designer.

I still remember her face when I tapped into this strength for the first time. "So, do you think you can design me a dress to wear to my friend's wedding?" Her smile expanded and her calmness exploded into a volcano of excitement. "Yes, yes, yes! I would love that! You would look great in green. What kind of wedding is it? Long or short?" Her questions were endless and her eyes sparkled with the delight that she was being acknowledged for her talent, which she believed in.

Often when somebody is stuck in a negative situation that is out of their control, like her mother's impending death, it takes great courage to celebrate what you are able to offer the world despite your challenges. She did this with open arms and although I didn't end up wearing her outfit to my friend's wedding (thank goodness not because she is now divorced) we dreamt up big dreams together. Mapped out pictures and explored fabrics. This distraction was a way to ease her feeling of losing control and it worked. In fact, it helped her to process her impending grief by channeling herself into her creativity.

There is power in giving ourselves permission to be sad

Our weeks together were fruitful and we were making steady progress. Mom seemed to be gaining strength and she had a distinct glow that had replaced her once yellow palour. The girls were getting on well, they were positive and there were no more unruly outbursts at home. Then the call came.

I was away on a trip in Cape Town, sitting on the water's edge, having a lunch with my husband's work colleagues from Belgium and Holland. Sunny blue skies, not a breath of wind. It all seemed so surreal to be hearing the voice on the other end of the line tell me that mom had passed on suddenly after being admitted to hospital with a respiratory infection. "The girls asked for you. They won't speak to anybody else." It was only when the unknown voice made this desperate plea, that I entered coach mode again and started formulating a plan of action.

When I next saw the girls, it wasn't in my usual coaching space, but in a bright, friendly, bustling restaurant chain for a chocolate milkshake. Looking back, perhaps this wasn't the right thing to do, but at the time, I thought it best to distract them from their sorrow so that they were forced to hold it together.

"I know mom is watching over us, and we will make her proud." said the once sullen 10-year old. Her older sister wrapped her arm around her lovingly and I knew then that they would be okay. Mom had prepared them for her departure and although I wouldn't be there for their future milkshakes, I knew that the seeds had been planted and that mom would oversee their growth from heaven.

Many of us are scared to talk about death, particularly with children, but it is an inescapable fact of life. Talking helps to alleviate their fears, misconceptions and worries and making the unknown seem more comfortable. Talking of course will never take away all of the pain, but it certainly helps to process it.

Talking our way through grief paves the way for healing

We have to realise that children become aware of death long before they are ready for it. They see dead birds, insects and animals on the side of the road or on their walks in nature. They may see death at least once a day on television. If they are watching cartoon network, no doubt they have seen the brutal death of more than one cartoon character in their time. By speaking the unspoken truths about death before crisis strikes adults can prepare children mentally for dealing with their upset.

Communication is key to everything and sugar coating the truth like this beautiful Cancer ridden mom had tried to do didn't help her girls. It just made them resentful and angry at her. She was well intentioned but her fear that her daughters would falter under pressure was unfounded. It turned out that these two were strong and resilient as a result of their mothers death. They faced the world with their heads held up high after their moms funeral. Just like their mom had done on her first visit to me.

She had left a legacy to last a lifetime. She departed in a dignified manner that paved the way for others to remember and respect her for the powerful and intelligent woman that she was. Death did not get the better of her because she gave her two beautiful daughters the most selfless gift ever. She gave them the skills to cope when she was gone. Watching down from heaven now, I am sure she must be proud.

Their dad and other family members were also instrumental in supporting them through this time. In fact they were surrounded by many people who offered help and extended their hearts and hands to help. Their home was a train station of support, with people in and out delivering condolences and frozen lasagna.

The view that the girls shared with me after their mothers funeral, was that nobody seemed to care about them after the actual funeral. Everybody had brought their dad food for a short while and so many people had visited their home because their mom was dead. At the time they had yearned for privacy to mourn and the interference of the well intentioned adults checking in on them and forcing them to say they were okay, really wore them down. However they felt that when everything had settled, there weren't many adults left to support them or ask how they were.

Protecting children from grief is not a productive way for dealing with the natural progression of life

I feel privileged that I was one of those adults that mom had put in place because she probably knew the truth behind her death. There would be those in it for the long haul (many of them because they didn't have a choice) and those that would superficially be around when it suited them. There is space for both, but out of the mouths of these two girls it was confirmed for me that they saw straight through adult pretences.

Respect is about being consistent in our offers for help. Don't say you will be there for a child when the going is tough and then disappear the moment you perceive them to be okay. This is why I coached the girls during maintenance sessions for a year after their mom's death and then gently sent them on their way. Content in the knowledge that they would be okay.

Like this client of mine, my husband's dear school friend passed on after a long struggle with Cancer at the untimely age of 45. He left behind a beautiful and accomplished wife and 3 young boys. What I remember clearly as we paid our last visit to him in the hospice where he eventually succumbed to his illness, is her sharing how she had broken the news to their boys that their dad may never go back home again.

Her tenderness and care in sharing the full truth with her boys about their dad's Cancer left me in awe and filled with great respect. Although those boys will no doubt still face tough times, as any child would who loses a parent after a traumatic illness, they will be okay. I know this because by whispering the unspoken secret out loud, mom and dad had empowered them to process their emotions and prepare themselves for any eventual outcome. More importantly, her words were grounded in a deep faith in God who was her steady anchor in her time of greatest struggle.

Faith in a higher power is a steady anchor in times of struggle

Speaking the truth about hard things is never easy. In fact, it takes more courage for an adult to face the facts even when it would be easier to sweep them under the rug. So many children who lose their parents to death or who watch their loved ones wither away from terminal illness are not afforded the respect they deserve. Adults should acknowledge that children are often stronger than we think and it is those very small innocent souls that may actually help us adults process our grief.

It is the knowingness of a parent left behind after the death of their spouse, having to wake up and keep on going because their children rely on them that is actually the saving grace. Parenting is a dual relationship between adult and child and nobody has all the answers when it comes to death but what my coaching taught me is that for any child to overcome their sadness, they need to be given permission first of all to be sad.

How many times do we as adults not acknowledge our own feelings. How many parents who are grieving go and cry in a closet because they don't want their children to see their tears. What is that telling them? That emotion is not okay? That being sad is wrong? In fact to the contrary, if we show children our sadness it gives them a platform to show us theirs. Would you want your child to hide in a cupboard when they are sad? Would you want them to not show their grief when they lose somebody they love?

I would love to wrap children in cotton wool and protect them from the sad things in their little worlds but that would be selfish of me. I do agree that life is unfair. Cancer is unfair. Losing a parent to death is most unfair. Losing trust because we don't speak the truth about death and how it makes us feel, is even more unfair.

It may be perceived as "cruel" of me to say this but I can't help but feel that children need to face pain in order to experience and find their inner strength. We underestimate how strong children really are. They are wise and all knowing. We owe it to them to tell the truth about those things that may change their lives in indescribably painful ways, but will set them up for a life of authenticity and openness.

Reframe your outlook and children will always follow your lead

Living in fear of death is normal. Death in itself is scary. At my uncles funeral, my niece age 3 was sitting on my lap. She was visibly distraught at the time and more so when leaving the church and seeing my parents - her grandparents - crying. She didn't understand the grief but joined us in our sadness. She sobbed her heart out, with her little arms holding tightly to my dad's neck as he did the same.

My nephew, her brother aged 8, had been sitting with my cousins children at the back of the church and when I saw him, his eyes were swollen with grief. He had been crying and we allowed him the luxury of doing just that. Without judgement and without feeling we needed to protect him.

My uncle died in tragic and unnatural circumstances through suicide and that is a conversation adults will still need to have with those two beautiful children that I respect as if they are my own. But for now, my family will just keep answering their questions about death when they pop up. Because they have and they will. The event was traumatic and if we don't speak about it, they may process it incorrectly. I would never want them to be fearful of death. I simply want them to respect life and all that it has to offer while we are alive and able to enjoy it.

Channel your fear of death into inspiration to make each day count

I once read that there are two great days in our lives. The day we are born and the day that we find out what we were born to do. Like this beautiful teen who was passionate about designing clothes, if we channel painful emotions into creative outlets the journey becomes so much easier. I am not in contact with her today, but my hope is that she has realised her dream of being an international clothing designer. I hope she has lived out her purpose that was voiced to me in our coaching sessions. If not, I know the seeds are at least planted and she has the tools to water them.

Who said death had to be serious? Why can't we draw, splash, paint, climb, build and have fun during the grieving process. Wearing black to a funeral is a sign of respect but how lovely would it be if we nurtured a "rainbow wardrobe" kind of thinking where children saw death as an untimely celebration of sorts. With the funeral being a party for the person they love in their send off to heaven. Imagine the departed loved one smiling down from heaven then!

For many years I put myself through the excruciating pain of long work hours because I felt I wanted to live my purpose before I died. I was always trying to prove myself. Sometimes I forgot to live because I was so busy creating my legacy. I neglected the ones closest to me and I forgot about the small things that are just as meaningful. Preparing for death is about living life to the fullest. Not over compensating or trying to prove our worth.

We need to coach children to be mindful of their time on earth and help them to make small incremental choices that relate to appreciation and gratitude for where they find themselves. The good and the bad, the happy and the sad all grouped together are the best teachers in life by far.

The Hidden Truths about death:

- *Being sad at times, is normal. Being happy all the time is not. Finding a balance between the two is a good lesson for children.*

- *Grief is something that needs to be processed. It doesn't have to be done in a serious way but a celebration can help just as much.*

- *Hiding the truth about death does not prepare children for the eventuality. Preparation is about finding acceptance within ourselves that we will cope whatever the outcome.*

- *Adults sometimes feel the need to protect their children from the hard things. It is in those times that children can have their biggest growth.*

- *Over compensating and over achieving while we are alive can wear us down. Celebrate the small moments along with the big to make your life meaningful.*

- *Finding our true purpose is about exploring what we want people to remember us for. Waiting to do this until it is too late is the regret of many people who are laying on their death bed.*

- *We all have a part inside us that years for acceptance. It is only in making peace that we need to accept ourself first that we will find what we seek.*

- *Happiness is an end result of a mind fulfilled. This doesn't mean there will never be sadness. It just means that you need to blend of the two into something harmoniously beautiful.*

- *Having faith when things are unexplainable and hard is important. It is in your lowest and most challenging moments that this anchor will see you through.*

- *Creating a legacy is about having a servant mentality. It is about giving the best parts of ourselves to make the world a better place before we depart this earth.*

8

THE DIPLOMAT WHO MISPLACED HIS SON

Hidden Truth:
Money should never be a substitute for love

"I don't have any friends because I'm too clever," was the first thing that this 13-year old said to me when we met. Followed shortly thereafter with, "My IQ is 162, which is technically higher than Einstein. I can play the piano, violin and drums, I speak 3 languages, have my own horse and do show jumping. I play golf with my dad on weekends and I will be going to an internationally renowned university to become a medical doctor."

Well, I didn't see that one coming. My immediate thought was to label him as a genius kid with a lack of social skills but I knew better than to do that without delving deeper into why he was actually being sent to me. My coaching space had just become stuffy as his once silent mom started crying, not just the sniffling quiet kind of crying, but the kind that left mascara running down her face, sobbing and scrambling for tissues in her bag. She cried more than she spoke, she just sobbed the entire time we were there.

The Genius Kid was an only child and his dad was a foreign diplomat who constantly travelled and was never home. Mom was a lawyer turned house wife who had apparently met dad on holiday at a luxury resort abroad, before he became a diplomat. According to her they were happily married, according to her son, they were not.

"Mom, you know that dad is never home, how can you say we are happy?" She wiped her tears and replied in a calm controlled voice, "We live the life most people only dream of and dad has given us that. Show some respect." I knew then that there was an underlying current that I would have to avoid tripping over if I was to succeed in my mission to deliver mom's request - to help her son make friends.

In that first session, there was nothing I could say that could convince Genius Kid who had been fast tracked two grades to "employ" me as his coach. He rigorously interviewed me despite mom's visible embarrassment coupled with her never-ending stream of tears. According to his self-created "genius" checklist, I wasn't qualified enough to be his coach.

"Can you tell me why you don't think I am qualified enough?", I asked. He stared at me as if to say was I daft actually asking the question. His mom, who was obviously used to his faked self-confidence and his attempts to manipulate adults because of his high intellect, stopped him with a simple hand gesture. It was a power move that needed no words and Genius Kid knew better than to continue, it seemed. That action showed me that mom still had some of her lawyer left in her, even though she appeared fraught with anxiety at being in a life that relied solely on supporting her husband's and her son's needs.

Dissecting the truth can eventually lead to multiple answers

With him finally listening to me, I proceeded to shift the power imbalance by getting to know him better. What I found out very quickly was that his mind had matured but his inner child still remained intact. His intellect had simply not allowed him to enjoy his childhood and this was the problem he was facing. It also didn't help that his parents put pressure on him to be the best at everything that he did. No wonder he didn't have friends, he didn't have the time! His days were consumed by endless tutoring, studying, attending sports fixtures, and practicing his musical instruments and multiple languages.

Making friends can be hard for any child, but for socially awkward gifted children, the challenge is usually multiplied. Their brains are, most of the time, working on overdrive, and they are confident enough to have an intelligent conversation with an adult expert in their field of interest, but put them in the same room with children their own age, and all bets are off.

Even as adults, fitting in and building relationships is tough. It's hard for all of us, young and old. Social dynamics have so many unwritten rules and for the most part we all fear rejection and want nothing more than to be liked. Finding the right friends for this Genius Kid seemed an impossibility and from what I was seeing it was making his mom unhappier than it seemed to be making him.

He seemed content in his own skin and although uniquely "weird" in an endearing kind of way, he appeared not to mind that he didn't fit in. He said he was lonely, but he felt he was coping. I knew he was hiding something and I made it my mission to find out what it was.

A lonely child can also appear to be confident in an attempt to control their environment

I can say with conviction that he was the child who spent the most time dissecting what I coached him in each session. Although at the time it didn't feel that way, I was making a very positive impact. He was internalising the tools and techniques of my coaching model on a higher level than I had seen in a child of that age before.

We had many stimulating and sometimes philosophical conversations about the research he had done after each of his coaching sessions. He studied up on neuro linguistic programming, and was especially interested in social psychology, which wasn't surprising since he struggled to make friends. During his time with me, he claimed to become a major fan of Martin Seligman, the father of Positive Psychology, and spent time sharing quotes or excerpts with me relating to happiness.

Sometimes, I secretly felt intimidated by his wealth of knowledge and my feelings often switched between being the confident, self-assured coach who 'knew my stuff', and the quietly insecure teen who, in her final year of schooling was told she was stupid by her guidance counsellor.

Yes that actually happened. Not in those exact words, but it happened in my final year of school when I was suffering from one of the many bouts of depression that would haunt me in the years to follow.

I had been diagnosed by my doctor as having "Glandular Fever", which is known to trigger depression and as such I was off school for a substantial amount of time. This resulted in my school marks declining, and as a consequence, my confidence too.

The pressure to lead can distract you from problems bigger than yourself

From an early age, I was singled out as a leader, which to some may have been an accolade, but for me it became a chore, a job, a task, that was flung onto me without the skills to handle it. I have held many leadership positions, from being Head Girl both in Primary and High School, to being elected to the Student Representative Council at Teacher's College for three consecutive years. I found all of these to have unbearable pressure as their common denominator simply because people pleasing was the drug of choice that made me feel good.

As a novice leader, I experienced the shame of being dropped kicked by the stress and pressure of life that every teen faces as their rites of passage. The problem was that I didn't cope, because I had a predisposition to anxiety and a low stress tolerance, and this, coupled with trying to always do the best and be the best, was a swift and sure way to spiral me out of control. I think that my family doctor hid the real truth though, and my symptoms, although seemingly indicative of Glandular Fever at the time, were painfully similar to those of the many bouts of depression that came after that supposed illness.

I was living two lives during that time. Angel on the outside, rebel on the inside. My week was punctuated by diligent studying, handing homework in on time, and being part of the "good girl" group, but my weekends were shimmering smoke screens of late drunken nights in clubs without my parents' knowledge, sleeping too little and partying too long.

All of this was fuelling my mental demise as I played yo-yo with who I was. Teenage years are filled with experimentation, and often the reward is far more important than the risk. I know my story is not unique and this is evident in research that shows that despite educational efforts to provide teens with information about risky behaviour, they continue to engage in it.

Although I was a good student, I under-performed academically as a consequence. I certainly wasn't a genius, but when my guidance counsellor told me that being a child psychologist or teacher wasn't a viable option for me, I couldn't help but disagree with her.

She proceeded to tell me I should rather consider secretarial options. At the time, had I not had the support of my mom who had been a teacher and a role model for the career path I was considering, I may well have believed her. How I would have loved to have had proper coaching at that career decision making stage. Unfortunately, I got a counsellor who wore two different coloured shoes with two different coloured knee highs to match.

There are many 'dream stealers' like her out there that dispense unfounded and unwarranted advice that crush young people into submissiveness. All too often, I have seen children settle into mediocrity simply because the adults who advise them keep them small. My wish is for all adults to see value in children dreaming big and to encourage them and fill them with hope, rather than use unrealistic academic standards to measure their potential.

Changing our mind is often a sign that the hidden truth wants to emerge

Half way through our coaching programme, Genius Boy told me that he had changed his mind and wanted to study to become a psychiatrist, rather than a medical doctor. He told me that too many teens were suffering from depression. This was my cue:

"Do you think you are depressed?". His answer came as swiftly as a reflex impulse. "Yes." Just one word that encapsulated the inner turmoil in this young man. How had I not realised this? Being a high achiever myself, and constantly striving to gain the approval of others, I, for the first time was able to slip on his shoes.

Although I was by no means as academically gifted as him, I could feel his pain. In fact I, relived mine through his. That feeling of overwhelm, anxiety and sleepless nights. The long hours crying many tears under a duvet in muted tones for fear of my parents hearing me, nobody knowing how I was truly feeling.

Just like me, he had the need to impress the adults in his life. This came from a yearning to be accepted. To be liked. High achievers often put pressure on themselves based on the feedback they get from others around them. With every good intention, parents who praise their child for the outcome and not the effort, set them up for a lifetime of always having to prove their worth.

I was never short of encouragement but it was almost always based on getting good grades or for something I had achieved. This led me to unpopularity in many ways. Although I had a tight knit group of close friends and would have been considered popular in the traditional sense, I was actually a loner just like Genius Kid.

Over achieving can be a mask for internal overwhelm

I didn't disclose my true self to my friends and they saw me as confident and driven when in fact I was just an insecure teen with a mind in disarray. I constantly put myself down and didn't believe I was worthy of being liked.

As a consequence, I haven't kept many of my school friends and in fact, this caused me to side step many friendships well into my adult life. It was only when I started loving myself, that I made lifelong friends who also love me for me.

We had much in common and Genius Kid's disclosure was the first step to him acknowledging his feelings just like I had needed to do as a teen. Something he had never had the luxury of doing before, and something that I had never been able to do either.

He realised that he had no need to impress me. I was not concerned with his musical ability or whether he could speak 10 languages. I was merely a neutral bystander who once upon a time had felt a small element of what he was feeling. I was equipped to get the best out of him socially and emotionally and so I left the intellectual stuff up to him and went about my work as best I could.

Depression comes masked in many ways. Adults sometimes are not aware that their over achieving child is masking their true feelings. By being busy and on the go, this distracts others from their inner turmoil. Often they self-harm in the comfort of their own private domain or binge eat or fill up on self-loathing without anybody ever knowing.

The truth is that many adults walk around with blinkers on. Not because they want to but because they are conditioned to do this. It is a self-preservation tactic that silently whispers, "If my child is okay, then I am okay." What they don't acknowledge is that their child may be struggling and by them ignoring the obvious signs, they are actually participating in a form of denial and perpetuating the problem.

Medically, a doctor would diagnose a child as depressed by looking at a variety of symptoms. They look at changes in eating with fluctuating weight loss or gain. Sleeping habits that show continual exhaustion and lethargy. Being irritable and grumpy. Low mood most of the time. Lack of interest in things they usually found stimulating. Less social interaction. There could also be physical symptoms like tummy pains, headaches and muscle tension. Grinding teeth, clenching jaw. Inability to concentrate and poor performance in school. Self-harm or, on the extreme end, suicidal ideation.

Depression is a reality that sneakily hides behind smiles and likes to masquerade as if all is okay

So how does one tell if a child is depressed if there are none of those tell-tale signs? What if the child has become so accustomed to functioning even with the dark cloud that they keep a secret overwhelming their mind? Would you have suspected depression in this Genius Kid who was admired for his discipline and drive to achieve, but who inwardly was devastatingly self-critical and relentlessly demanding on himself?

While high-functioning depression doesn't look like the stereotype of depression most of us hold in our heads, this diagnosis nevertheless carries significant risks if left untreated. I had missed a few tell-tale signs that Genius Boy had masked very well. He was overly critical of himself and others. Remember the initial interview when he said he didn't think I was qualified enough to be his coach?

Clue number one right there. Then, clue number two was his constant need for perfection in a household of parents that condoned perfectionism.

The shadow side of his constant striving was how unrealistic the demands were that he made of himself. Clue number three was that he was constantly psychologically beating himself up for falling short of the goals he set for himself. Let's be clear here, these goals were by no means your average achievements and so it was easy to fall short. The thing is that he achieved most of them and still, for him, it wasn't enough.

Mental health struggles come in all shapes and sizes and great work is being done globally to undo the stigmatisation of mental health issues that society has scripted over the past few decades. Unfortunately, children slip under the radar because most people still have an unconscious image in their heads of what a depressed person should look like. Genius Kid and myself when I was a teen, looked nothing like the traditional depressed person.

"Holding it all together" behind the smoke and mirrors of achievements made it hard for Genius Kid to admit he needed help. His mother had spotted his inability to make friends as a reason to solicit my coaching advice but the very real mental and emotional strain he was under simply flew under the radar.

Mental health issues are often not noticed when there are too many distractions

The good thing about our coaching sessions though was that through his personal growth, he managed to gain the belief that with enough effort and willpower, he could achieve, gain or fix anything that life threw at him when supported.

High-functioning depression is a biological and psychological disorder that requires adequate and clinically appropriate treatment. If left untreated, it can potentially bloom into major depression. The reality is that with high-functioning depression, (I know from experience) moving through your days can feel like you're attempting to build a castle on a foundation of quicksand.

What I know now about my depression as a teen is that I managed to somehow get through. I had suicidal thoughts, but never acted on them. I did act out though in other ways, through binge drinking and late night parties without my parents knowledge, as a way to relieve my stress.

Genius Kid on the other hand was protected because his dad was high profile and he was seldom allowed out of sight of any adult. His safety was paramount and so his privacy was not respected as it traditionally is in more mainstream households.

He asked me, in fact he begged me, to please not tell his parents what he had disclosed to me. Unfortunately, in the best interests of his safety I was obliged to report his depression confession. With his permission, I set up a meeting that included him, with both his mom and dad. This was to discuss a plan of action for moving forward.

Mistakes can be productive if we learn from them

Although I had made good progress, he did not want to terminate his coaching and nor did I feel it was the right time to do so yet, I still felt it best that I refer him to a psychologist for a proper psychological assessment and a possible treatment plan to complement my coaching programme.

Sadly it didn't quite work out as I had expected. It was a unique situation because dad was a very busy man and although his wife had reminded him about the meeting, he called at the last minute to cancel because of a "work emergency". This was after the original trio of myself, mom and Genius Kid, already assembled.

Personally, I think dad may have forgotten about this meeting because his cancellation call was very strategically placed. The truth is that dad was not present for his son and all he yearned for was a father figure who cared about him and not only about his achievements. Genius Kid didn't want his father's token gifts of expensive holidays, a thoroughbred horse or playing golf on the best course. He wanted what money couldn't buy. I see this kind of unintentional neglect so often in the upper demographic clients I work with, and it is no wonder Genius Kid felt the way he did.

At around the same time as Genius Kid, I had a similar case of lack of parental involvement with another client. I was running a four week family programme, and in the first and last weeks, parents are required to attend. This is mandatory, and I always make that quite clear on sign up because it is one of the reasons why my programme is so successful. Through using a whole family approach and establishing roles and responsibilities within the family in the initial session, we have a foundation to build upon which we can then consolidate in our final session together.

So when I was approached by a well-dressed man in a black suit and tie with a backdrop of snow white shirt to register two boys in my programme, I at first thought it was one of the fathers. I soon learnt that this was the family chauffeur and due to the fact that mom had become busy, he had been tasked to attend the family workshop with the boys.

Not only was this embarrassing for the boys, but their mother missed the entire point of the workshop which was that they share family bonding exercises. Needless to say, she did make the effort in the final week after I stressed the importance of her attendance. Their dad, it seemed, was unavailable and not involved, and I still secretly commend her on stepping out of her comfort zone.

She was a stark contrast to the other casually dressed parents, as she sat on a bean bag with her tailored designer pencil skirt suit and stiletto heels, immaculately manicured nails, salon perfect hair and a professional glossy exterior of make-up. From experience working with parents like this, I knew this was merely her shield to the world.

By the end of the session, she had tapped into her inner child and it was a joy to see the way her boys leaned into her spark of adventure and fun. Her heels had taken flight and, hair dishevelled, she participated in every activity with reckless abandon, eventually forgetting about her carefully put together exterior.

Going back to basics could be the solution that was always in plain sight

There is a great lesson to be learnt in this - that sometimes children just need their parents to be present in the right measures at the right times. Just showing up is often enough to give them a clear message that they are worthy and that they are deserving of your time. For those two boys, the first week of agonising embarrassment with their chauffeur was redeemed by a mom who realised that she had let them down. It is never too late to make right as a parent if you feel your children have missed out on a part of you because you strive for money or something else external as the core ideal. The real growth comes in acknowledging that you may have messed up and then stepping up to the task of salvaging your relationship at the expense of you having to admit your own mistakes. Money simply cannot buy that love.

Money is a poor substitute for love

Usually I spend months with children goal setting, getting them to dream big and mapping out a plan of action to work on their lifestyle. Genius Kid was different. He knew exactly what to do and in what order and in what measures, so we approached things differently. I coached him on how to be a child again. We built puzzles, painted pictures, moulded clay and crafted designs out of beads and wire, all the while giving him the permission to just play again.

So often, the solutions are right under our nose and for Genius Kid it was no different. All he needed was to have somebody take the pressure off him and I was that person. When he was in my company he didn't have to impress me with his high intellect, accomplished vocabulary and multitude of achievements. He could just be the young teen boy that he was meant to be. He spoke about girls and the awkward shyness he felt when approaching them. He started making friends because he learnt to take an interest in what other teens were doing and not only speak about his own interests.

In short, I can say he was a delightful boy who reminded me of my own depression. I too had felt like him as a teenager, minus the genius! He brought out my desire to see a world where every child has a 'tour guide' to hold their hand through the ups and downs of life. It isn't bad parenting, neglect, abuse or any of those things that have the strength to knock a child down. What destroys them is when they have no hope and they don't know how to overcome victim mode and step into their power. Kids Life Coaching is the perfect support system in a world where children are often left to figure things out on their own.

"You are clearly destined for greatness. I have no doubts about that," I told him in our last coaching session. Then I asked him a question that I asked all of the older children I coach: "How are you going to create your own legacy?"

His answer is to this day cemented in my mind because of its sincerity. "I want to be like you." My look of surprise triggered a cheeky grin on his face. "I want to leave every person that I meet with a random act of kindness. That is the only way to make friends with the world. To expect nothing in return."

Hidden truths about money:

- *Children want what money can't buy. They want an adult's time and attention to the smaller details in their life.*

- *Spoiling a child with toys, gifts and money is a sure way to numb their sense of appreciation if this is done without the lessons to value what they are given.*

- *Being successful in life is not associated with how much money you earn, or what job you have. It is about being a good person who cares about others.*

- *The real meaning of being a genius is not associated to IQ, but to having a healthy Emotional Intelligence.*

- *When children see adults value material things over relationships, they will do the same.*

- *Even those with all the money in the world still have issues. Earning cash does not entitle you to a problem free life.*

- *Affluence is best enjoyed in the company of those you love. Being rich can be a lonely place if you stand on the heads of others to get there.*

- *Real wealth is not measured by your bank account. It is counted by your health, relationships and how you impact others with your time.*

- *Life is counted by the number of moments that take your breath away. Often these make the best memories and cost the least money.*

- *Never sacrifice family or friendships because of money. Many relationships are broken because of this.*

9

NO BUILDING TALL ENOUGH

Hidden Truth:
Suicide happens because of a loss of connection

"I am going to kill myself and I want you to tell my family that I love them." I remember his barely audible voice. It was crystal clear with determination. In my years of being a Kids Life Coach, this was the first time I had experienced a distress call of this magnitude. I had stopped coached this young man a few years prior when he was in his mid-teens, yet he had chosen to speak to me. Surely this was a cry for help?

I remember it being a cold and dreary Friday night in Johannesburg. It was raining so hard that my husband and I had decided to buy take aways from our local drive through. We were in the midst of rolling out the first step in our stay at home evening of delicious chicken dinner coupled with wine and a movie snuggled on the couch, when the crisis arose.

Although I had all the skills necessary to deal with this, my fear response clicked in as I instinctively deduced that he was serious about his threat. "I don't believe you. If you were, you wouldn't be calling me." This brought no response. I continued to chastise him according to suicide protocol to find out more about his intentions. The fact was that he was in crisis, but had decided to tell me, was in no way an indicator that he wasn't planning to go through with it, so when he eventually spoke, giving me specifics, it was also a very sure sign that he was in deep trouble.

"I want you to look after my brothers like you looked after me." At the time, perhaps, this may have been construed as his compliment to me, but it was shrouded in expectancy and half truths that he still had a shred of reason and will to live. He didn't want to die, but at that stage, he had lost hope.

I remember when I first started coaching him as a teen, that he was a determined young man - a real leader who paid no heed to the naysayers who labelled him as a trouble maker. He was simply misguided in those days and after going through my coaching programme, he had managed to rebrand himself and find his true worth. He excelled at school and ended up in university in a chosen career path that related to psychology. So the conversation we were having was surprising to say the least. I had not seen it coming and nor had I expected it from this solid, self-assured and confident young man.

Build relationships with children so that they will come to you when they need it most

I believe in maintaining contact with my coaching clients after they have finished my coaching programme if this is possible. He was no different and we often caught up for what I call "maintenance sessions". These check-ins allow me to reinforce the skills my coaching clients know already and to remind them of the value of the mental toolbox they have in their possession. I knew during this call that simply reminding him of these tools was not going to do the trick. This was a crisis, and demanded more solid and focused attention in order to achieve a short term outcome. That outcome was to keep him alive long enough to change his mind.

"Okay, so tell me how you are going to kill yourself?" I remember speaking with faked disdain for the situation, frantically fighting the anxiety that was slowly constricting my throat. "Really, you know better than that." Still no response. "Are you there?" I remember cursing silently in my mind because he wasn't responding. I immediately stepped into blame mode asking myself "what I had done?" In that brief moment, I thought I had pushed him over the edge by asking for too much detail but it turns out that it was that specific act that saved his life.

If some in-between state existed, some other alternative to his death, I suspect at that stage he would have taken it. Motivation for suicide may not always be about attaining death because often for many it is more about escaping emotional pain or escaping from a bad situation. It's rare that only a single event leads to suicide and in the case of this young 19 year old, I knew that he had been through tremendous obstacles that I had coached him to overcome. What I was hearing in his very calm voice was an underlying helplessness and hopelessness that had obviously pushed him to this point of seeming no return.

At the time, I had never been truly suicidal myself, and had only ever entertained thoughts of it, but never wanted to follow through, so I had no idea what it felt like or what I was dealing with. I had done courses, read protocols and educated myself on what to do when counselling somebody who is suicidal. Little did I know when speaking to him, that only a few years later, I would be feeling exactly the same way. I too would be truly suicidal and my lifeline would be knowing I had talked him out of taking his own life. In essence, he saved me, but at the time neither of us knew this.

Mistakes can kill you
if you let them

My coaching style had always allowed for an open and honest conversation but I sensed that this was not quite what he needed. It seems like he intended to go through with his threat and I felt like I had merely been carefully selected as a messenger. In fact, if anything, his lucid and calm approach gave me all the more reason to believe his claim that he was about to take his own life, because of what is commonly termed as suicide exhaustion.

After intense inner struggles, the sense of relief at knowing all will be over soon, is a perfectly logical reason for the calmness. He confirmed this with me by saying that he actually thought this was a solution to all of his problems, so therefore there was no need for him to feel upset or agitated.

Until much later I didn't know his reasons for this extreme measure, but at the time I did know that in general, young people try to kill themselves for a variety of reasons with the most prevalent being that they are depressed. The second is that some are impulsive and often this is linked to the use of drugs and alcohol. The classic one of course is that the teen is crying out for help, and they don't know how else to get it so although they don't usually want to die, they want to alert those around them that something is seriously wrong.

Young people who are looking for help often don't believe they will die, frequently choosing methods they don't think can kill them. The final reason and the one that turned out to be the case in this young man was that they've made a mistake.

The definition of a mistake is: *"An action, decision, or judgment that produces an unwanted or unintentional result."* Now in the case of this talented and intelligent young man, he felt that the end result of his choices gave him no other option but to pursue death. He felt he had messed up his chances and there was no redeeming himself.

There are three key motivational aspects which contribute to suicide. These are: 1) a sense of not belonging, of being alone, 2) a sense of not contributing, of being a burden 3) a capability for suicide, not being afraid to die. All three of these motivations or preconditions must be in place before someone will attempt suicide and this young man confirmed this in his conversation with me on that cold, rainy night that I will never forget.

Life is a sum of our choices

The tagline for my organisation (that supports children around the world through coaching) is: "Where choices are made easy." This is a perfect way to sum up the process of coaching that enables children to actively consider their options and to choose their outcome based on their next move.

We are a product of the choices we make and each decision helps to define who we are. All of us are confronted by countless choices every day, some of which have minimal consequences, and others can be life changing in the split second that we make them. Suicide is that life changing decision that has a point of no return and can define a person after their death by that one moment of choosing to give up.

My cousin, aged 29, dramatically escaped from life after he shot himself on 6 January 2018, barely one year after my uncle (his dad) did the same. At the time it didn't come as a shock to many of our family members because they said they were expecting it. They had seen the signs. They had watched his demise as he grieved his father who had left him, his mom and younger brother with debt and little income from their family business.

He had been in an alcohol fuelled fight with his fiancée which had pushed him over the edge. His split second decision could have been eliminated had he picked up the phone and spoken to somebody rather than pulling the trigger. He was a sensible young man with a kind and generous heart. How I wish he had called me. But he didn't.

He had been admitted to a rehabilitation facility for alcohol and sleeping pill addiction just 7 years earlier under the supervision of my husband and I. We were so proud of the fact that for years he remained clean, but life threw him one too many curve balls that caused him to make errors in judgement and he started drinking again. Everybody could see his life as a recipe for disaster but nobody was able to intervene.

Our perceived mistakes are often our most valuable lessons if we choose to learn from them

In the months preceding my cousin's suicide, his message to me was consistent. As I counselled my own family member, with as much objectivity as I could muster, he confirmed that he didn't belong and that nobody cared about him. He was of the opinion that after his dad's death, many people simply faded into the woodwork and their original offers of help were unmet and never honoured.

He also told me that he was unable to step into his dad's shoes. No matter how hard he tried, he felt like he was letting everybody down. Lastly, being a keen and avid hunter he had no fear for using a rifle. This was the final contributing factor to his death. He had access to the means and wasn't scared to use it. I so wish he had made another choice, but he didn't. I do know, however, that this final act of defiance to life itself does not define him and I don't judge him for it.

Making good choices begins with taking charge of the decision-making process and being content with where you've been, where you are now, and where you're going. It's about being proud of who you are, what you represent, and the impact that you're having on others. This begins and ends with the choices that you make.

So when we make what we perceive as mistakes, this has the ability to impact negatively on our inner worth, which can create unhappiness because we have acted in a way that has denied our inner truth. Perhaps the most fundamental consideration with choice-making is to ensure that the choices made are congruent with important goals, which is what my Kids Life Coaching process is about.

Pause for reflection when you feel overwhelmed

Much of my career is about identifying and supporting children who may be at risk of depression. In the last few months of my cousin's life I knew he was at risk and I counselled him as best I could from the UK with him living in South Africa, yet at that split second moment he only heard the one voice in his head.

I feel guilt even though his last words to me and mine to him on were "I love you". We said it to each other often and it gives me joy to know he knew this. But my love didn't save him. He made a choice in a moment that will forever leave my families hearts' empty and confused. For some, maybe even angry at his perceived selfishness and his "error in judgement".

What I learnt through my cousin's suicide is that we should not ask why. It is not our job to make sense of why somebody makes the choice to die. After it has happened, it cannot be changed, and it is about moving forward and cherishing the lessons that can perhaps save somebody else in future.

When we understand the dynamics of choices, this can help improve the decisions we make. Essentially, any choice involves at least two options, both of which have pros and cons and it is a skill to become comfortable with trusting that we are making the right choice. Ordinarily we're very good at making choices with the easy things and we do so efficiently and seamlessly. Now and then, however, we come up against a decision that forces us to pause for deeper reflection.

Coaching children to view every decision they make as a stepping stone on their pathway in life helps them to remain consistent and congruent with the goals they want to achieve. When my client told me he was choosing to die, I knew this was not consistent with the goals that we had set for him and that he had made such remarkable progress at working towards.

I remember that telephone conversation with my client so clearly because it was his calm and measured words that unsettled me so much. He seemed so convinced that suicide was his only option. He sounded so convincing that at the time I could feel the adrenalin rush that contributed to my usually calm composure crumbling.

It was in that moment that I knew I needed to pull myself together for the sake of supporting this young man who at the time seemed clearly intent on acting on his words. They were simple, succinct and convincing, "I am going to jump." This was the little clue that saved him that night.

I transformed the role of messenger that he had designated me with to the one of detective and possible rescuer. I made it my highest priority to gather data, and I knew it was imperative that I acted fast. When on the phone to somebody who has just admitted they want to take their own life, the first thing to do is to find out where they are. "Are you at university?" An affirmative. This was my second clue.

I had stayed in touch over the years doing coaching maintenance sessions telephonically or via Skype when this young man needed a little boost, so I knew that he had all of the skills for picking himself up when he fell. I had coached him to understand the dynamics behind positivity, using focused future orientated thinking, seeing the bigger picture but most importantly, making choices based on what is in the heart and not in the mind.

Even strong people sometimes need somebody to lean on

He had a toolkit and I needed to remind him of that as his coach, but at that point, also as the person that could potentially save his life. There are seven key ingredients that I coach children to actively set goals on implementing in their lives. These are eating, sleeping, exercise, leisure time, education, communication and support. This list makes up the recipe essentials for maintaining mental well-being, so I knew that somewhere on one or more of these ingredients, this young man had faltered.

By contacting me, he was implementing the ingredient of support, if perhaps only on a subconscious level. This is the most important default ingredient when all others are out of sync and I hope to believe that perhaps the fact that I had coached him to understand that even the strongest people need support, was indeed the underlying reason that he was speaking to me.

In the case of my cousin who took his life, he was burdened with a mental illness, a disease that was in plain view to all of us who knew him. If he had cancer or diabetes, perhaps many would judge him differently. I refuse to judge him by his destructive behaviour that was merely created and perpetuated by his illness and the choice he made to take his own life.

Could I have done more for my own family member? Possibly. Could all of us as a family? Maybe. Yet I feel strangely at peace that his pain is over. The hidden secret of his mind in chaos that held him back from achieving his true potential is now in the open. He is the reason I am writing this book after procrastinating for so many years. He inspired me to act on my dreams and whisper my own mental health problems out loud in the hope that this can help others.

His struggle with depression ended, albeit in a way that is not congruent with happy endings. He took that into his own hands. When his whole world was falling apart he took control over the one personal thing none of us could ever influence. His right to choose to die. Nobody could understand that but I do. I get it.

Suicide doesn't kill.
It is the lonely dark days leading up to the act that do

In my darkest days of being suicidal, I envisioned how I would complete the act, yet I would go about my days as if everything was okay. I would do my daily chores by rote. Completing my tasks on a neatly ticked checklist, all the while having multiple pictures in the back of my mind as to how I would take my life. I had conversations with myself trying to convince a part of me that I was being unreasonable because I was so supported and so loved but a dark cloud of depression has a way of drowning out even the loudest and most reasonable of messages.

I know now that it takes great strength and resilience to push through when you only see darkness where there should be light, and my cousin had the ability but he was tired. I was once tired too. So I know how that feels.

One trigger eventually pushed him over the edge. I believe that my cousin's story is no different to so many others. No different perhaps to your own story. No different to mine. He was thrown challenges he didn't ask for like the death of his beloved father, my uncle, only 11 months prior to his suicide. This pushed him over the edge and was the contributing cause to him to make bad choices like drinking alcohol when he had been clean for so many years. Regret at his choices. Being pushed into a corner. Being judged. Feeling unsupported. Giving up. That is what drove his final decision.

Suicide doesn't kill. It's the dark days that kill off the soul in the time leading up to the act. It's the small daily events and struggles that he couldn't cope with, that robbed him of the freedom to choose to live a full long life like he was meant to. Depression and the demons that go with it made him believe nobody cared, that he was not worthy, that he was better off dead. It's the voice in his head that lied to him and hid the real truth. That he was supported and loved by me and his mother, his brother, our big family, friends and work colleagues. That he was worthy of help. That he could get better. That there is strength in being vulnerable and asking for help.

Coping with an inner struggle is easy when you have a support network

Looking back now on that traumatic conversation with that young suicidal coaching client, I realised that our strong connection was forged in our coaching sessions. Somebody I had never grown up with like my cousin and didn't know like the back of my hand, had asked me for help. This cemented my belief that Kids Life Coaching is a worthy modality that can save lives. Even in the line of work that I do, with all the things that I know through my experience and education, there is a fine line between reason and delusion.

My cousin didn't have my resources, so I cannot judge him on his decision. I just know that so many young people can be saved if we lay the foundation for being the leader of their own life at a young age.

That stormy night, with my ex client threatening suicide, I was so inept yet fully aware. I stated something to this young man that may have on the surface level appeared obvious, but in reality was little more than me trying to solicit more information. Still in line with my role as detective racing against time to solve the mystery of whether he was intent on acting on his threats, I told him "There isn't a building high enough to kill you. I don't believe you. Besides when do you intend jumping."

Making mistakes is part of life and learning from them is how we grow

If you ever receive a phone call from someone who is suicidal like I did, I recommend that you listen attentively to everything and try to learn as much as possible about what the caller's problems are. Staying calm, and being supportive, sympathetic, and kind is not easy but it is the fine line between life and death in a situation like this.

That night, in a roundabout way, I asked him the three most important questions that saved his life: Do you have a plan? Do you have the means? When will you do this?

I know now that I probably didn't use the right words at the right time, but what was important was that he understood my genuine concern that was free from judgement, because we already had a relationship from our previous coaching sessions. Research has found that simply talking about their problems for a length of time will give suicidal people relief from loneliness and pent up feelings, and give them a feeling of being understood.

Although I am a problem solver at heart, I avoided giving advice, or trying to negate the reality of how he felt that night. It is not how bad the problem is, but how badly its hurting the person who has it. I could tell he was engaged when he responded, this time without thought or hesitation.

I remember his message being garbled and it went something like this: "I really didn't mean to. I just took my eye off the ball. She was so good to me. What happened. Alcohol. Weekends of partying. Failed. I'm a mess. Look at me an idiot. Bad marks at uni. They all said they were my friends. I was drunk. I loved her." His words made no sense but I read between the lines to understand what he was saying.

Like so many of us, his life had fallen apart for a variety of reasons and the culmination was his decision to look for a long-term solution. It isn't that he didn't know any better but that he had lapsed in his judgement and made choices that he felt he couldn't bounce back from. In reality, if a young person, and especially a child understands that making mistakes is part of life and contributes to our growth, we wouldn't be losing so many kids to suicide.

I asked him, "When are you going to jump off this tall building?", hoping for a straight answer. A pause and then, "Now" he said. It was then that my adrenalin kicked in fully, rendering my mind crystal clear, and I scrawled the words "Call campus security," across a piece of scrap paper, coupled with the name of the university he was based at.

As my husband frantically made the call that could ultimately save a life, I tried to stay calm, but my brain could not decipher what I was to say next. The script wasn't supposed to go like this and he had thrown a noose around my neck and I knew that I was on the edge of hanging myself in terms of professional advice.

In the moment, I shelved the fact that I may have messed up and I tried to speak him down. "Do you remember the first day we met?" I said. Without waiting for a response, I continued "You were so angry, I was really scared of you." I gave what to me sounded like a low fake chuckle that seemed like I was having an out of body experience. "I am so proud of what you have achieved, you should be proud of yourself too. This isn't you talking, this is you against a wall and not knowing which way to turn."

Even a system meant to protect can let you down

I still hear that stifled sob on the other end of the line that signalled a turning point in his thinking. "You don't want to do this.

Just take a deep breath and think back to a time in your life that made you feel so incredibly proud. Can you see it?" I was just buying time, speaking aimlessly, trying to fill the void with words, in the hope that we could save him.

It happened while I kept talking. Without warning or hesitation, I heard him give a low deep guttural moan as a man repeated the words, "We are here now." over and over again, and then the line went dead. In that moment, I knew what I needed to do next, despite the imprisoned tears that were at last escaping the confines of my eyes.

My husband drove me to the university as I sat in a haze of tears to match the heavy rain pelting down as a worthy opponent. The wipers were working overtime, and so was my heart. When we arrived, we were led to a small room, where he sat staring blankly at the wall with the Fire Exit safety instructions curling at the corners behind him. When he saw me, he let out a sigh of relief and my doubts that he really wanted to die, evaporated. I knew instinctively that he wanted to live, he just didn't know how at that moment in time.

That night became a blur of telephone calls to his parents who lived 6 hours away by car, asking for permission to intervene. I learnt then, that if you show no visible injuries externally, an ambulance won't take you away. It was for this reason alone that my husband and I got permission to put him in our car and drive him to the nearest hospital to get help. My husband always being the practical one put the kiddie locks on the doors in case he decided to jump out of the car in another suicide attempt.

I was so shocked at the complacency of the university who sent nobody to his aid and wanted to send him back to his student residence. It was after working hours and it seemed nobody was available to intervene in crisis on a Friday night. I am not sure what suicide protocols are at other major universities, but I saw first-hand evidence of how the system let him down. I have heard of high suicide rates in many universities and I wonder if it is because they feel unsupported? It seems with valid reason.

Eventually in the early hours of the Saturday morning, we got him admitted to a psychiatric clinic after the local hospital said they didn't have a bed for him because he was suicidal. I spent hours speaking to doctors in low muted tones and constantly reassuring him that he would be looked after. As he drifted into a drug induced sleep, I said a prayer that he would be okay. I was his Life Coach all those years ago, yet he had chosen to speak to me. The basis of the work that I do is first and foremost about support and everything is secondary to that.

Showing your authentic self is your greatest asset

There are many useful suicide helplines and I had called two that night to get help for clinic referrals. They are usually manned by volunteers and I really honour the work that they do with very little resources and what appears to be inadequate training. If only we had a world where a call centre for suicide wasn't necessary. Where governments saw spending funds on coaching for children as a priority rather than investing into programmes or helplines that are reactive.

I have personally experienced what it feels like to want to die. I know what a lifeline speaking to somebody can be. Just like this client of mine, who eventually received the appropriate support he needed, only a few years later, I was also admitted to a psychiatric ward.

The difference between him and I are not only a vast number of years in age, but my education and understanding of the psychology behind suicide. Coaching should be preventative but I know that sometimes when our lives get chaotic and we face severe trauma our brain chemistry shifts and we need alternative means of support.

There is no good reason to die but there are many brilliant reasons to stay alive. I think one of the reasons so many children choose to die is because they know no other way. Nobody has given them a lifeline. Nobody has told them that no matter how big their secret is and how much they have messed up, there is always a way out. Life is about setbacks and challenges and it is in these moments that we experience our greatest personal growth. Some people may disagree with me, but if we shelter children from the storms of life and we don't allow them to really experience the highs coupled with the lows, we are doing them an injustice.

So many children lose themselves in the overwhelm of the pressures they face. I have spent so much time coaching children through a variety of pressures but there is always a common thread. Every single child no matter what they are facing has the need to be accepted unconditionally.

The reason they don't tell the adults who love them when they mess up is because they feel like they may be judged as a failure. They avoid the admonishment because they don't want to disappoint the people they love.

With me, as a coach, there is no disappointment. Just reflection. I am simply the mirror that shows the child that their mistakes are not a sign of their true worth. What really makes them valuable members of society is admitting when they get things wrong, learning from their mistakes and using those to do better the next time.

Mistakes shape us into who we were always meant to be

Adults make mistakes all the time, so why then are children so scared to do the same. I simply think it's because adults hide their truth. They don't show the warts, bumps and bruises to the children who love them. They strive to be "perfect" in every way and modelling this negates the fact that we are all fallible as humans.

We are all learning beings who are navigating this thing called life as best we can. Rather hold hands with children and tell them our truth because there is no use in hiding our biggest lessons. I am not saying that we should disclose everything inappropriately but what we should do is have an arsenal of our own "failure" stories to support children through their own.

Life is about getting back up once we have fallen down but it is just so much easier when there is somebody there to lend you a hand. I would not be here today had it not been for so many people in my life who encouraged and supported me through the dark days in my lustreless void.

I know now that I needed to walk that road myself so that I could share it with you. My hope is that you will take this message and build a foundation of support in the children you care for most. They don't want you to be perfect, what they want is for you to be unconditional. Why is it that children tell practical strangers like me their biggest secrets? Because there is no judgement.

Be the role model that a child needs by talking through the ups and downs together. Stop keeping secrets that could be the greatest learning opportunities. Find ways of communicating your mess ups that is safe and satisfies the need for acceptance but allows for personal growth.

Hidden Truths about suicide:

- *Show your authentic self to children by sharing your successes and your failures. This way you give them permission to get it wrong occasionally.*

- *Depression doesn't cause suicide. Not asking for help when you need it most is the main catalyst for making an irreversible decision based on a temporary situation.*

- *Children need unconditional support when they make mistakes. This doesn't mean accepting their mistakes without repercussion. It simply means giving them a lifeline when they need it most.*

- *If adults feel overwhelmed by life, then imagine what it is like for children. The way to support them is to equip them with the practical life skills for dealing with challenges.*

- *Pampering and protecting children from the harsh realities they may face will not help them in life. With every good intention, an adult who keeps "life truths" from children is doing them an injustice.*

- *When a child faces an adversity out of their control, this could be the catalyst for their greatest personal growth. Resilience is born out of pain and experiencing that pain.*

- *Coaching children to ask for help when they need it most could be a life saver. There is great strength and courage in admitting defeat and being willing to accept support.*

- *Suicidal thoughts are a reality and often an objective view is needed for taming that unreasonable voice that could be the fine line between choosing to live or choosing to die.*

- *Children should be given a toolbox for positive mental health.*

- *Preventing depression is more valuable than trying to get rid of the side effects when it is too late*

10

STRIPPED TO THE BONE

Hidden Truth:
Your job title does not define you

She was a cliched blonde bomb shell. One of those women who turns heads when she walks into the room. A tight butt, big bosoms and succulent red lips framing her long false eye lashes that were curtains to her deep green eyes. Her face at a closer glance looked slightly weathered with age, but her body told a different story.

I envied her toned stature that was a mirror version of an athletic 20-year old but she must have been at least double that age. I had met her briefly at a business networking event after opening my third Kids Life Coaching space when my husband was transferred from Durban to Johannesburg to open his own new office.

I had initially been sad to leave the sunny blue skies of my coastal home town to greet the dusty cosmopolitan city of gold, or Jozi as it is affectionately called. However I was feeling an excited anticipation for the first time since arriving as I sat around a table with 8 other business owners. The buzz was electric and the dynamic was different to my sleepy home town where doing business was a paler shade of grey. It seemed that inland, people were more driven to achieve and their hunger for it was evident. In fact it was so evident that it was contagious and I felt inspired to achieve more simply because I had changed address.

So when she joined our group, finally closing the gap and making us a table of 10, I knew the night was going to get interesting. She spoke in animated tones and made determined eye contact as she fluttered her eyelashes at the doting men at our table. The other women, myself included, paled in comparison to the sex appeal she oozed. On her arrival, we all just made general chit chat until we got to the part of the evening where we had to introduce ourselves as business owners using our 60 second pitch.

Judging a book by its cover can be deceiving

The real aim of me attending the evening was to get new coaching clients for my personal practice. At that stage, I had trained and employed a young part-time coach who was also a practicing psychologist. She helped me to pick up the work load simply because I was eager to service the need in my community and my time didn't allow me to do so by myself.

I was also keen to drive more foot traffic through my doors as I was preparing to showcase my business model as a franchise, which could be easily replicated. In fact I wasn't quite sure of how to pitch myself. Despite this, business talk came easily to me since I was young, confident and passionate about what I did.

I couldn't understand then, why around this lady, I seemed to splutter and splurt and my words stumbled into a string of incoherence. I felt intimidated and wasn't exactly sure why. In fact, I knew from her demeanour that she had money - lots of it - but that wasn't my issue. My real issue was how uncomfortable I felt when she shared her profession.

I now look back on this event as a turning point in my mindset. It was the start of my journey to shift my once judgement fuelled thinking that a person's career defines them, to a neutral gear. I always try to be fair in my interactions with people, but not so much when it comes to anything relating to child neglect, abuse or wilfully bad role modelling where I seemed to take personal offence.

I am not sure what entitled me to be the self-appointed "child protector" but I was a spokesperson for anybody under the age of 12 and my fiery opinions were well backed by research and fact. Why this sexy lady rattled me, I didn't know, but she did. I think it was because on a personal level, on that particular night, I was needing to learn a lesson and Sexy Lady was about to teach me what that was.

"I am the owner of a strip club. My girls are clean and I screen them personally. I consider myself an expert because I was once a dancer myself."

I think the men at the table were in awe at this fantasy come true but the women seemed rattled by the shock of it all, and a deafening silence fell on my ears. She giggled politely, "I always get that reaction, but you will see I'm just normal. My body is a canvas and my girls and I are in the entertainment industry. All above board and meant to satisfy a natural need that is as old as the ages."

After disclosing her occupation, of "exotic dancer and strip club owner", I felt an immense fascination, and for a short while we broke from the 60 second pitch format and allowed her more than her allocated time. I joined the interested men in asking her questions, the rest of the women shuffling uneasily in their chairs, checking their manicured nails, coughing under their breath or readjusting their hair, all of their behaviour illustrating that they felt intimidated and lacking in approval.

I am not sure why I eventually settled in and found her easy to talk to. Soon I was entangled in her quirky entertaining mannerisms that consisted of well-placed hair flicks, pouting lips and the odd cheeky seductive smile that had a confident knowingness to it.

She was comfortable in her own skin and I had a strange admiration for her. You may wonder what caused that, but she really sweet talked us and her words glamourised the industry. Her elaborate descriptions of weekly doctor's checks, drug testing and being a "mom" to her girls seemed to add a touch of class to what I had always judged a sleazy industry.

So when everybody's eyes fell on me, as it was my turn to pitch next, I felt my stomach flip. I simply did not want to be the person next in line to speak after her. In fact I couldn't think of anything worse since our industries were so starkly contrasted. I was like the North Pole and she was the Sahara Desert.

Remembering your true worth
can be hard when you are in a minefield
of temptation

When I was a teen, I was nicknamed Ice Queen because of my ability to stand up to a boy's seduction. I was one of those girls who finished my schooling still a virgin even though I had a steady boyfriend. She seemed like the girl at school who earns a reputation for being 'easy' and has no qualms shifting from boy to boy as a hot and sultry commodity.

I commend myself now, but my pitch wasn't half bad because just like Sexy Lady, I brought curious questions and lots of interest. But, here is where things got really interesting. Most of the questions were being posed to me by Sexy Lady and she seemed genuinely intrigued by what I had said. She agreed with my opinion that children need good role models. She agreed that with the modern day influences, children were at risk. She agreed that children were losing self-esteem at a rapid rate. In fact, she was like the ideal parent excepting that like me, she didn't have any children of her own.

The questions she was asking were on behalf of her 'girls', the strippers who worked in her club. I was fascinated by the fact that many of her employees not only earned a pension fund but were also mothers.

She spoke with great admiration about her 'girls', who danced night and day to pay for their children's private schooling, guitar lessons and first cars. Many were single moms and Sexy Lady felt passionate about serving them.

It was then and there that she hatched an idea. It was to offer me a gift, not only of a steady stream of clients, but the gift of the most interesting clients. She said she was going to pay my fees, and money, she announced, was no object when it came to her 'girls'.

I couldn't believe that I had just picked up what could be termed as my first "corporate contract", although not entirely mainstream. She said she had never heard of Kids Life Coaching before and just like weekly doctor's checks, she thought it imperative that her 'girls' get the parenting support they needed.

I was fearful that I wouldn't be able to deliver at first but then something came over me that I suppose was me rising to a massive challenge that could prove to be most meaningful.

Morally and ethically everything she did went against my beliefs. I didn't agree with her profession. I thought it tacky and pitiful that she made heaps of money from the seduction of young toned girls flaunting their bodies to horny old men.

Yet I knew that there was something genuine about her if she was choosing to pay for her staff and their children to attend my family coaching programme. So I chose there and then not to judge. I set aside my personal moral beliefs and saw this as an opportunity to not only make a difference where it may count, but to be paid well for it too.

We all get a chance to dance in the hall of shame

In the months that passed, she was true to her word and I had multiple new clients from her strip club. They would usually arrive in zippy little sports cars, with their well-groomed children in tow, not offering any clue as to their chosen career path. One particular mother however was slightly different. She seemed less impressed with the money and the glamorous lifestyle and more concerned with the well-being of her two children.

She arrived each week in a taxi, with her pre-adolescent son and 9 year old daughter. The difference was that she always brought her mother with her. Unlike the other ladies who spoke proudly about their career path in front of their children as if they had studied for years to be a lawyer or a doctor, she hid the truth.

She was insistent in briefing me to do the same and she warned me that her children did not know what she got up to for her job. She reassured me that this was only a temporary measure and that her children deserved a good life after their father left her for another woman. She was barely thirty, so I estimate she must have been a teen when giving birth to her son.

Her mother, the granny to her children, knew of her daughter's sacrifices as an exotic dancer and she was very supportive. They had an exit strategy and they saw me as the biggest opportunity yet, to successfully navigate the quicksand of the stripping industry she found herself in. Our coaching sessions together were punctuated with the occasional tears as this caring mom became emotional at the wasted opportunities in her own life.

We became a tight knit little team in my jovial coaching space littered with brightly coloured bean bags which were a strong contrast to the dark sultry atmosphere of her work place.

After 7 months of working together, I had seen a steady incline not only in her children's attitude, but in her own self esteem. Her once spoilt children who seemed to take her endless pots of money for granted softened at the edges and I opened the lines of communication and enabled them to repair their broken bonds caused by mom's personal issues, of what turned out to be a school girl pregnancy followed by abuse at the hands of a man she thought loved her.

Her low self-esteem was a precursor to her children's bad behaviour and my intervention had cured their bad habits across the board. I can only hope that my coaching had served to break the cycle of poor self-image that probably led her to pursue a career in exotic dancing in the first place. Who knows as I never saw her after that final day when she hugged and kissed me goodbye and got into the taxi with a sad wave of knowingness that all would be okay without me.

Opening the lines of communication is about being honest about your intentions from the outset

The Sexy Lady paid the bills for a while and then she stopped. I called her to find out why, but she just evaded the question and to this day I don't have the answer. Being curious, I googled her website at the time of writing this book and came across this post on her job seekers forum:

"I'm a 23 years old black female, I am really interested in being a part of your lounge club. I'm a mother of 2 so I just needed to know all the requirements and benefits if I qualify to be a part of your club."

I guess that word is still out on the street that she offers good benefits for moms and that she looks after her 'girls' well. I can only hope that she still does and that this job seeker who wrote this post, manages to provide for her two children not only with abundant financial resources, but also with the seeds of self-love.

Although I feel strange admitting this, the biggest question I never did get to ask was what these 'girls' filled out on their children's school registration forms as their occupations. I wondered how many of the top private schools in Johannesburg were aware that the money that paid for the best teachers in the industry was earned through taking clothes off and entertaining business men who could very well have had children in the same school.

I suppose this is the cycle of life, with money simply being a currency of exchange for perceived value. At that stage, the salary of these dancers per month was the same as the average government school teacher's annual earnings.

Achievements without values intact are not worthy of celebration

The hidden truth of what I learnt within this strip club industry, was that money is a driver for making choices that are not always aligned with long-term interests. The moms I worked with, except for the one who had verbalised her exit strategy, seemed to place more worth on material possessions for themselves and their kids than they did on earning an honest wage.

I wonder if this is caused by the seductive lure of commercialism that tempts us with the newest gadgets, the latest fashions and top class holidays. I don't think such massive sacrifices in personal integrity are limited to exotic dancers. Although they don't take their clothes off, how many parents take jobs that rob them of their true values and leave them as poor role models to their kids with only lies to tell as the history of their life?

Whilst all of the women I met were beautiful and worked hard to keep their bodies in tip top shape, they were broken inside. For them, the dancing seemed to be a drug that cured their lack of confidence.

One of the girls told me that she felt like a movie star on stage and that she loved the adrenalin rush she got before her sequence. She particularly enjoyed the rich men who threw money at her and propositioned her for sex. Although she didn't give in, as this was strictly not permitted in this particular club, she did disclose that her exit strategy was to find a rich man to marry. I wonder if she did and I wonder if their children today know how their mom and dad originally met.

I cannot deny that although I learnt not to judge these mothers, I did feel a tugging sadness in my heart. I couldn't help but feel that they were victims of circumstance who perhaps never had a role model in their own life. They were doing the best they could with the resources they had available and their most valuable commodity was their body. Their currency of exchange was undressing in front of strangers. This afforded them a similar lifestyle that a university degree and 20 years in the work force as a lawyer could buy. All because they were gifted with a gorgeous face, worked hard on sculpting their body and oozed sex appeal.

The under belly of the hidden world can swallow you whole

I remember spending a Friday evening watching a documentary screening with a friend, that followed the story of young girls trafficked into the sex slave trade. Whilst this strip club was by no means that extreme, I can't help but wonder how many were merely channeled into the industry by the behaviour of the adults around them.

During this time, I remember having a distinct sense of unease as I couldn't help but deduce that some of these dancers may have been victims of sexual abuse. They had never felt the respect they deserved for their bodies and so they willingly shared the most sacred parts of themselves with the very men who didn't deserve to see them.

Perhaps their beauty was a poor substitute for brains and so they saw little other option. For them, their aspirations exceeded being a cashier in a supermarket and although their choice can be frowned upon, what they did do is provide a better life for their children than they had ever had.

This particular strip club had bill boards all the way down a main road in my old suburb and I remember one of my clients who had a regular day job complaining about it. She admonished the women who sold their body for money.

"Trash I tell you. These sign boards are polluting my children's minds. How do I explain this to them?"

What a good question. How does one explain this kind of choice that an adult makes. The one that sees them willingly overstep the boundaries of socially acceptable decorum because of their apparent lust for money and the lifestyle that goes with it.

This is not limited to the sex industry, but what about the child who has a parent who sells drugs, or is involved in a gang or is a thief? What about the child who has a parent who is a government official who takes illicit bribes? Surely all are as bad as each other.

As a teacher many years prior in one of the most elite schools in Johannesburg, I now look back and try to visualise which parents were involved in illegal trade, whether of their body, guns, drugs or otherwise.

Although exotic dancing is not illegal and Sexy Lady reassured us that night around the table for 10 that her 'girls' never did more than dance, I wonder how true this is. What is the tipping point for parents who become greedy? How far will they go to provide for their children? Will they make choices that will forever haunt them as secrets that can't be whispered out loud?

Choices that have to be kept a secret were never good to begin with

It is the choices that adults make that require strict safe keeping in the heart and mind that do the biggest damage. How many children know of their parents' illicit trade to earn money and follow in their footsteps because it is the only thing they know how to do? Although I no longer judge these parents, because they all have their reasons, I know that their choices are not based purely on survival.

A mother who begs on the street with her toddler munching on an apple while she collects coins to pay for a night in a hostel is cut from the same cloth. She has also been hurt, perhaps abandoned, perhaps abused like the ladies in this club. Yet, even with her beautiful face, she would never consider placing her toddler secondary to her money earning capacity. She sees the days on the street protecting her child as days well spent. Dancing in a club while a stranger looks after her kin is not an option. She would rather struggle than make a choice that could end up haunting her for life.

Perhaps you are going into preachy, judgement mode right now. I am sure you have your own opinions, but the fact remains that any parent will do what they need to do for their kids based on their own set of values. If we are to break the cycle, it starts with coaching children to embrace a whole new set of life principles to live by - where children see self-respect as the core aspect of their existence, where taking their clothes off in public for money wouldn't even be a consideration.

I know I am naive to think that the derelict mind of our underworld can disappear overnight, but surely it starts by educating our kids. Telling them the truth about the lure of commercialism and the thrust for us as humans to compromise on our values because we want to be part of the "rich man's club". I want more for children and I will do my utmost to break the cycle wherever and however I can.

So, the next time you see one of those ladies in the queue in front of you, I am sure you know the type I am talking about - her wafts of perfume a seduction to match her skimpy clothing with two kids in tow. Stop wondering like I used to, if she is a good mom. Just accept that she is doing the best she can with the resources available. It is not our job to judge her but it is our job to inspire the children that we have a direct influence over.

I want you to consider this. What if you happened to be that child? Like the children that I coached whose mothers were strippers. What if you knew what your parent did for a living? Would you be ashamed of your upbringing and the choices your parent made? You see, the fact is that your parents don't define you. They may shape you and instil their values in your mind, but ultimately as an adult the final choice is left up to you.

I encourage you to whisper the secret out loud that so often needs to be heard. That negative cycles can be broken and that your past need not determine nor destroy your future. So often, children are victims of their parents' negative choices but this doesn't have to be the final word in the matter.

Children judge their parents by the quality time they invest into them

Being ashamed of a parent for the job that they do, is hard for a child. I think any child if asked, would rather have a parent who cleans toilets and has a good solid set of values, than a parent who is a government official and doesn't care about the well-being of others, especially their own family.

I think most children don't really care about the job their parent has or how much money they earn. What really counts is the small in-between moments that they spend together as a family. So often, career driven parents choose their job over their family and spend more hours with their work colleagues than at home. What is the hidden truth behind that message? That strangers and money and power are all more deserving of their time?

Children who have parents involved in illicit trade still deserve to have hope. There is always hope, and just because a mom was an exotic dancer, a dad a pimp or an uncle a drug pusher, it doesn't mean that this child can't one day win the Nobel peace prize.

It is in the strangest of places that we find hope. Being stripped to the bone and bearing our true values without hiding behind the hidden truth is what makes us human. Mistakes and choices need never be permanent. It is always a choice.

The Hidden Truths about Careers:

- *A job title does not define who you are. Your values and how you treat people is the true determining factor behind this.*

- *The best leaders are those who are not obsessed with their career progression, but who see the importance of building their own life and family first.*

- *A person who does not earn as much money because they lack in intellect or skills is still worthy of respect if they are doing the best they can with the resources they have available.*

- *Parents sometimes make decisions for their children based on giving them a better life. If this is based purely on earning capacity, eventually the cracks will start to show.*

- *Learning the value of life is not about salary, but about the positive impact we make on the lives of others around us.*

- *Low paid labourers have the ability to think the same way as high powered executives. The difference is in how confident they are at playing the game of life.*

- *Judging others who don't fit the status quo is short sighted. Every person makes decisions based on their personal circumstances, which are often hidden.*

- *Sometimes parents need to trust that their child's career path may be off the beaten track. This is okay if based on what is in the heart and not in the mind and done for the right reasons.*

- *Many people yearn for respect and acceptance, prestige and wealth. Not everybody attains this but some that do sacrifice their personal integrity along the way. It isn't worth it.*

- *Children who are proud of their parents, feel that way because of how they make them feel, not because of their career choice.*

11

EMPTY VESSEL FULL OF SAND

Hidden Truth:
Labels do not define true potential

In 2012, I found myself on my first overseas business trip to Canada, that allowed me to meet a remarkable little girl. My Canadian colleagues had arranged for me to present some workshops in their local schools. I had expected to meet a host of school leaders who made a positive impact on me, but that little girl shone like a shooting star on a dark night. The truth I saw is imprinted in the story of my mind and she gifted me with the ability to see past a child's label with conviction.

On this particular school visit, the principal greeted me with a big smile, telling me that '*his*' children (aka I'm in charge of this school) were ready for me. I was hustled into a colourfully decorated classroom, and was rather surprised to hear no "kiddie noise" as I liked to call it.

In my teaching years, my absolute favourite was to hear the children having productive group discussions in the classroom or to hear squeals of laughter and high pitched voices playing games during break time.

This classroom was different, with an anxious group of serious looking 6-year olds sitting quietly with their fingers on their lips. All of the children except one. The little girl with neatly braided hair sporting two colourful ribbons, wandered the classroom aimlessly, picking up a pencil here and there, turning a page in a dog eared book, knocking some Lego blocks off a desk.

As I prepared my book, puppets and music, I stole glances towards the girl who had now stopped to stare out of the window. The other children still sat quietly with fingers on their lips and seemed to be oblivious of her presence. The principal, teachers and teaching assistants all ignored her and so I immediately assumed that it was going to be my job to get her onto the carpet to enjoy my story time.

You don't know what you don't know

I started sifting through a myriad of labels running through my head: *Attention Deficit Disorder, Autism, Asperger's.* I forced them to the back of my mind.

"Sweetie, I'm about to start and I would love you to join us." She didn't even acknowledge me and as I'd predicted, also gave me no answer. So, I turned my attention to the other small statues on the carpet, "Well done children, for sitting so quietly, shake those fingers out and let me see your big smiles!"

I had the ability to quickly build rapport with children of any age, through my subtle jokes and easy mannerism that always put them at ease. I could see their bodies relaxing, as I played them a music soundtrack. This brought an animated response as some of the children got up to dance and others clapped and sang out loud.

I should mention that I once walked the red carpet for the 17th SAMA (South African Music Awards) with the producer of that CD. We were nominated in the top 5 Children's Music Albums in 2011 and I even featured in one of the tracks. The very talented producer had insisted that I sing in the chorus of one of the songs even though I don't have a voice that I ever considered recordable. It just goes to show that when somebody pushes you out of your comfort zone, you can achieve things you never imagined possible.

As the lyrics permeated the air, the children wiggled their bodies in unison, expressing their delight at the sabbatical from fingers on their lips. I then realised the real truth behind this seemingly well-behaved class. Their unusually good behaviour was by no means a reflection of what they were really like behind their closed classroom doors. They were what we term in the teaching fraternity "challenging kids" and the teachers and principal had probably threatened them to be on their best behaviour because I was a visitor.

Ruling by fear is a self-serving way to control children

I could tell that they were used to being ruled by fear which is so often the case when teachers are unable to control behaviour in a mass setting. So, my positive interest in their spontaneous participation was met with a further eagerness of the kids to interact with me. With my behavioural management experience, I had no doubt I could reel them back in again, but would I be able to do the same with the Day Dreamer girl, with the pretty hair, framed by glazed over eyes?

As I walked over to her, I could see the staff whispering behind their hands, and not knowing what they were saying, I took this as an affirmation to pursue my goal. When I touched her shoulder, she barely flinched, "Can I race you to the carpet?" This brought a small spark of a reaction, but still not enough to engage.

"Okay, get ready, get set and goooooo." I shouted loudly. In slow motion, Day Dreamer turned and scuttled her way to the carpet. The only left over spot was right by my feet tucked up close to my mini chair. I invited her to sit next to me and without hesitation, she took me up on the offer.

I could see that she was uneasy and rather edgy, so I placed a soft spongy stress ball in her hand. This was my long-time companion that was a winner when trying to elicit focused concentration from children. She willingly accepted the gift and with my gentle nudge of reassurance, I continued with my planned workshop.

By this time, the previous little statues of submissive good behaviour had turned into hulking monsters that were rough and tumbling, pulling hair, making silly faces, shouting and teasing each other. My stomach did a flip as I realised the implications of failing this 'test'.

My teacher hat that was accustomed to unruly behaviour, quickly fell into place. I stood on my chair and started clapping my hands. Not the kind of wild clapping you hear at concerts, nor the kind of restrained clapping you see at gala dinners. This was a game that the children immediately wanted to play.

"Right," I said, holding my arms out to the front shoulder width apart. I started moving my arms up and down in opposite directions "Every time you see my hands meet each other, I want you to clap." A momentary look of confusion but as I commenced the 'game', the kids soon got the hang of it and in no time at all, they had calmed down.

Disrupting a child's normal routine can lead to chaos and overwhelm

By this time, I hadn't noticed that Day Dreamer with her braided haired, pretty face, and glazed over eyes, was still sitting quietly on the carpet periodically squeezing my stress ball. She was watching me with deliberate intent and I knew that we had connected. Using her as an example, I pointed out to her peers, "Can you see how well behaved your classmate is being? She is sitting quietly on the carpet and listening to me. Show me that you can do the same." The rest of the class looked pie eyed as they stared at me with semi-confused expressions.

What transpired was something I will never forget. One by one, as if by cue, the rambunctious children sat down on the carpet as if somebody had flipped a switch, almost like little robots running out of battery power.

Their transition back to their former submissive state was almost instantaneous and I thought at the time that their teacher or principal had given a silent signal to them. I knew from my days in the classroom that teachers and children have an unspoken code that is signified by the raising of an eye brow, or the pointing of a finger, or a signal of the hand as if bouncing a ball, all to signify that it's time to settle down. What I didn't realise was that it was actually Day

Dreamer who was the silent signal they were unfamiliar with and they took it very seriously.

Finally I was able to start my workshop and since Day Dreamer had been such a good example, I asked her to help me with a very important job. She answered woodenly, "Okay", then glanced back down at her lap. She became my handy puppet helper and shared my colourful African Wild Animal puppets with her peers.

The looks of delight as the children became engaged in the moment, enjoying the sing song and dance was priceless. A little boy sitting to the rear of the class out of the blue bellowed, "Why does she get to help you? She never sits on the carpet." He was visibly upset and rightly so, if what he was telling me was true. I had no answer for him, but what I did have was a quick solution. "Honey, would you mind sharing your job with your friend over there? Let him hand out some puppets as well."

Day Dreamer promptly walked over to the boy and methodically and accurately gave him half the puppets to dispense to his class. The rest of the workshop went without a hitch and the children, although filled with the desire to move around after I had energised them, were also motivated to be unique and kind.

This was in response to my colourful rainbow Zebra character who is a loyal favourite of children. I created him to show children that they were born to stand out and be unique. Encouragement is his middle name and this unique Zebra knows the value of being the leader of his own life first, the lesson being that we cannot control the actions of others but we can control our own choices.

Raise your expectations and a child will meet you there

It was only much later, when I was having refreshments with a group of teachers in the staff room that I realised what I had achieved that day. They highly rated my workshop, which was an enormous accolade for my first international 'gig'. Not only had I equipped the children with the skills to practice mindfulness and exercise self-acceptance, and empathy for others, but I had achieved something I had never set out to do.

It turned out that Day Dreamer had been labelled with autism at the age of 3. She up until that day, had never sat on the carpet, nor uttered a word, or followed a full instruction or completed a task asked of her by her teachers. I was dubbed the "Child Whisperer" by the staff, who eagerly asked for some more tips for dealing with the little girl.

"All you have to do," I told them, "is enable the label." I further explained that since nobody had given me any confirmation that she had a label, I treated her just as I did the rest of the children. My expectations for her were high, but most of all, they lacked the condescending judgement and pity that many teachers seemed to buy into without realising this was what they were doing.

Day Dreamer had performed at her own personal best with me because she could. Not because she wanted to, but because she was made to feel "normal" by my inclusive practices. Momentarily, she was able to just be without having to stay within the confines of the low expectations that had been cemented by the adults in her care.

A child's performance is like a thermostat. When we want to adjust the temperature on the thermostat, whether it is higher or lower, it may take a while to reach the desired result, however once there, if we do not touch the dial again the temperature will remain constant. Even if the weather gets warmer outside or snow sets in, the thermostat will stay at the programmed result.

This is just like Day Dreamer, who had been programmed lower than her ability. She simply didn't bother trying any harder because nobody demanded it of her. Too many children fall into this trap because adults decide their potential according to a symbol on a report card or they compare them to the achievement of other kids. They never equip the child to step out of the pre-determined "thermostat zone" by giving them new ways of approaching things.

Labels are for things, not kids

There are so many missed opportunities when children are treated as incompetently competent. If that makes sense to you, well done but think of it this way if it doesn't - it gives many adults great safety and satisfaction when they can box children according to their behavior, especially in the classroom setting as this is a handy way of maintaining crowd control.

Sadly, this is one of the reasons I left teaching. I simply did not enjoy watching children being boxed and limited according to a few ignorant teachers' opinions. I was always the kind of teacher to go against the status quo and I think this comes from my initial foundation in my first three years of teaching where I was placed in a school for learning disabled children.

Going against the status quo at the right time will earn you respect from the right people in the long run

I had 11 kids in my Grade 5 class and all were on medication for hyperactivity (ADHD) or concentration problems (ADD) and other variations of the alphabet disorders like oppositional defiance disorder (ODD), obsessive compulsive disorder (OCD) and the like. They were tough kids, naughty and challenging. But at the time I attributed this to their myriad of labels and their genetic tendencies that the school psychologist and pediatrician had so aptly pointed out to me at the beginning of the new school year.

I remember my classroom as being the most vibrant and colourful in the school, and I spent the week prior to the kids arriving for their first day of school painting and decorating. The school was poor by traditional standards and had no budget for aesthetics but this didn't stop me from dipping into my own meagre funds saved as a teaching student, to make the space less institutional and more child friendly. I have so many interesting memories of what teaching in an establishment like this taught me and how it framed my experiences for becoming a respected and experienced Kids Life Coach.

One memory that always stands out for me is that they used to line up in the morning before class and it was my role to administer their 'daily fix' of medication to help them concentrate better in class.

I had no choice in this and this was merely part of my job description. I had a water jug and plastic cups and I religiously handed each child their prescribed Ritalin or Concerta saying a silent prayer at the start of each new school day, that they would have a better day than yesterday.

Why this memory has really stuck is that I could visibly see them change personality as the drug induced calm kicked in during the morning. It breaks my heart....because as at the time, I held an uninformed belief that they needed medication. I now know better and whilst in some cases medication is necessary, majority of the time it is simply a band aid for emotional distress or poor lifestyle habits.

It was in this first school that I saw the real immense problems these type of labelled children face. Their daily struggle to learn was a given, but more striking than that was the fact that they really struggled to interact. Socially they were inept and couldn't participate in sports or extra-murals because the teachers grew weary of their constant fist fights and taunting of each other.

Navigating life without a tour guide can result in getting lost and never being found

Navigating the unwritten rules of friendship, teamwork and discipline was a minefield for these kids who simply didn't understand how it all worked. The problem was that nobody ever took the time to coach them. I remember many passionate debates about their potential in teacher meetings. "You will learn." I was told as a young teacher. "They will let you down, so don't expect too much."

As a naive first year teacher, I was determined to prove them wrong so I embarked on a project to host a mini sports day and swimming gala. The first of its kind after being abandoned previously, because of jaded thinking about the effort required to execute the intention.

I see now, how to the older teachers I must have been exhausting with my endless energy and my optimistic outlook. I once heard some senior staff members whispering behind closed doors that I was doomed to fail at my venture. "She doesn't know what she's doing. Typical enthusiastic first year teacher", they said.

However, my principal had given me the green light and I was certain at the time she wouldn't have done so if she thought she was setting me up for failure. Luckily she was a good leader and really cared about the children, and her management team could learn a thing or two from her willingness to accommodate new ideas.

The fact that the majority of the school was medicated on Ritalin was a minor problem to me. The big obstacle I knew would be to get the children to participate as a team. To play fair. To win or lose gracefully. I poured my heart and soul into setting up the sports events and I am pleased to say that they were successful even though they were entirely non-traditional

With our fun family day kind of events like wheelbarrow races, sack races, and egg and spoon races. We even had doughnuts tied with string hanging from a tree with a race to see who could finish theirs first. The joy in my heart when I saw the originally complaining teachers make the effort by choosing a theme for their class and getting dressed up as a team, was immeasurable.

I truly believe that team work makes the dream work and I couldn't have done it without the eventual buy-in from many of the more caring teachers. The ones who, like me, still had the energy and loved the children to the extent that they would try anything new if it would be of benefit.

The difference between how I operated and how they did was that I was cheeky. End of story. I was open in my views and I always put the children first. This didn't curry me favour, but it did allow me to eventually be head hunted to work in a leading private school group as the youngest teacher in their history at the age of 25.

Children flourish when we respect them as unique individuals

This experience of seeing how the children flourished pushed my desire to do more to work outside the confines of their labels. So I also started an art project, raising funds through cake sales and raffles to buy supplies because our school funds were low. Those fund raising ventures were my claim to fame that I think set me up for my success as an entrepreneur.

Sadly, I remember walking into our newly renovated staff room after a holiday, complete with new couches and elaborately framed paintings on the wall. I had been told funds were short for art supplies yet upper management thought it was okay to spend money on non-essentials that ensured the comfort of those same jaded school teachers who didn't give the children the true care and consideration they deserved.

Just like Day Dreamer, these children were misunderstood, and they simply played to the expectations of their previous teachers. No matter the label, every child deserves to be respected and not judged. We don't know what happens behind closed doors, like the little boy in my class medicated for ADHD who found his father twice after an attempted suicide. He was ten.

Or the little girl of the same age in my class who came to school tired most days of the week because her mom was out partying and she had to wait in the car until she was ready to go home. This was child neglect at its worst in a social care system that couldn't manage their case load, so the education system drugged them instead.

It is no surprise that I learned early on that many labelled children - but not all - are usually a by-product of their parents' neglect. I loved the children in my Special Needs classroom and I could have been exactly like the other teachers, but I chose not to be. I chose to see the glimmer of hope shining in their eyes.

I met Day Dreamer long after I taught these children and so I was way more experienced in handling her appropriately because I had unraveled the incorrect teachings I had been given and reframed the way I saw labeled children.

Imagine a world without unconscious bias

Just imagine a world where teachers learn the skills for removing their unconscious bias as part of their initial training. Most teachers are dedicated to treating all of their students equally, but they can sometimes fall victim to the phenomenon of discrimination towards children based on their personal beliefs and experiences. This can most often be related to social status or gender roles.

Day Dreamer and the Special Needs children I taught, all had a commonality. They were different. They did not fit in. They behaved in a way that made them stand out. In short, they displayed challenging behaviour that couldn't be controlled by their teachers and so expectations were lowered to meet their needs as defined by their labels.

My real understanding and insight into the true meaning behind misdiagnosed labels first came when I took my precious Special Needs class camping in the wilderness!

My husband, my mom and I....with 11 "crazy cool" kids! I was told by my colleagues that I was mad to take these kids out....I insisted anyway!

Our class had won a school recycling competition and we had money to spend. In fact, we won most competitions, what little there were, simply because I spent lots of time and energy investing into "my" kids during school time.

I was a young teacher who spontaneously and intuitively went against the establishment and at the time my naivety was a true blessing to those children. I simply refused to accept and I questioned everything. I must have been a nightmare to manage because for me, the children always came first and there were never any exceptions.

This has never changed for me, and I simply do not accept 'rules' or 'diagnoses' simply because the professionals say so. I look beyond the borders of perception and make up my own mind in such a way that the child is always the outright winner in the equation.

Challenge the perception of what is wrong by focusing on what is right

That weekend we went away camping, I did not give my Special Needs kids any medication. This was with their parents' permission and I can tell you this secret - I had the best behaved children ever. Not one problem! None of the misconduct I was told to expect. My mom, who was a high school principal at the time and my loyal and involved husband, were unwittingly lured along to join me.

They saw the good in these kids like I did, although they did notice they had an overflow of energy. What was also evident was that their impulsivity slowed their reactions when it came to assessing dangerous situations.

Does this warrant medication? It was clear to me that a weekend in the wilderness expended the excess energy that wasn't conducive to classroom learning. These children showed me a different side to their abilities. If only we could adapt our classroom teaching to take place outdoors, to accommodate these "Ferrari style" fast thinking little minds.

The reason for their impeccable behaviour is that they enjoyed the refreshing change from their classroom struggles in numeracy and literacy. Outdoors, they were engaged and active. That weekend, we climbed, swam, rowed, sang, cooked and hiked together! There was no time for misbehaviour and nature was a perfect antidote to release their built up city energy.

The gift those kids gave me that weekend was immeasurable. After that, I started looking beyond what it meant to not be able to "concentrate" in class. I started researching and reading. I became a keen advocate for a medication free classroom.

I delved deeper into the psychology of the neglect and abuse some of the kiddies in my class were facing. I saw their emotional wounds and started really understanding the humanness behind their "bad behaviour". It was then that I first used the phrase "All bad behaviour in a child is a sign of an unmet need." This phrase has now become an integral part of the Kids Life Coach Training courses that I offer and is our mantra.

Shaming and blaming is not a tactic that gets sustainable results

Coaching children is about finding out what needs are not being met and then working towards supporting the child to better verbalise and get their needs met. As a Kids Life Coach in the business for decades, I always assess a child fully before agreeing with a diagnostic or medical label. I look at the 10 areas of their life that can impact on their performance and behaviour which cover everything from eating to sleeping, family dynamics, school and toxic environmental influences.

You are welcome to use this online lifestyle assessment tool on my website for yourself. It allows a pre and post assessment and gives a graphical representation of where a child's life may be out of balance. It then allows you the opportunity to bring the child's life back into balance by removing any undue labels and looking at the facts.

My Kids Life Coaching Tip to you is to always separate the behaviour from the child by exploring the bigger picture! Never buy in to what teachers or medical professionals say without first investigating yourself. You can easily get rid of labels simply by deciding to do so. Rather than box a child in with text book descriptions, give them the opportunity to flourish and grow in the fertile environment that you provide them with.

Always explore labels that a child has been given fully before buying into them. So often children are misdiagnosed because of symptoms that are very usually the cause of environmental factors. As an adult, you need to stay informed and act accordingly. Don't just listen to what the professionals tell you. Even if there is truth in their diagnosis, the fact is that they do sometimes get it wrong.

I have always walked the road least travelled and whilst it is easier to go with the flow and agree with the majority of the medical fraternity and what the Diagnostic and Statistical Manual of Mental Disorders says, I can't bring myself to conform. You see, children are so vulnerable and precious, and I feel that with the proper foundation in place at a young age, we wouldn't be seeing all the problems we are seeing.

So many children are victims of their environment, their parents, their school, their peers. I refuse to accept however that as victims they are unable to be equipped and empowered.

Children are remarkably resilient and whilst we want everything to be perfect for them, it will never be so. What I do know, though, is that you may be the person that saves a child's life from fitting into a negative mould that society gives them because of a series of behaviours that can be modified and changed through coaching.

Rebranding Childhood is about speaking about the labels that are stopping our kids from being kids. Be the one to separate the label from the child and give them a fair chance!

The Hidden truths about labelling:

- *All bad behaviour in children is a sign of an unmet need. It is up to us to find out what that need is and act accordingly.*

- *Judging somebody by a label they have been given is a sure way to lower your expectations and hinder positive interaction.*

- *Nobody deserves to be boxed in according to what they can't do. Rather celebrate their strengths and minimise their perceived weaknesses and classify them that way.*

- *The professionals sometimes get it wrong. Go with your intuition and ask questions before accepting a diagnosis that could hinder more than it helps.*

- *Forget about what the books say. If you feel that a child doesn't fit the label that a professional has given them, then remove it.*

- *So many children are incorrectly diagnosed with learning difficulties because of environmental factors out of their control. There is a difference between the superficial and real thing, so be aware of it.*

- *Teachers can be selfish, inconsiderate and lacking in empathy. Not all but some. It is usually those who have become jaded by the system.*

- *Trust is the foundation for any relationship. When this is broken because of somebody else's actions, you need to salvage your dignity by telling the truth.*

- *Labels are not an indication of a child's true potential. Potential is found in the things that cannot be measured in assessments, diagnostic tests and score cards.*

- *Many people fear being different. Yet it is in their difference that they can inspire others to step out of their comfort zone to do the same and make a positive impact on the world.*

12

PUPPET ON A STRING

Hidden Truth:
Failure doesn't really exist

The growth of my first business was exponential in a short space of time and I was a great success as a Franchisor, but I lost sight of my original vision and became bogged down by the daily administrative tasks involved. It didn't just happen overnight, but my confidence started diminishing as the loyal supporters (my franchisees) I had trained and nurtured with all of my heart and soul started pointing out, subtly at first, the perceived errors that I was making as their leader.

In my inner talk, this equated to flaws in my personality since I was a people pleaser and took their criticism to heart. Despite my outer façade of confidence and my natural ability to lead, I had always felt less than perfect and the negative input was not well received. I became stubborn and abrasive, fielding the seemingly endless complaints as one by one my franchisees started throwing 'excuses' at me as to why their business wasn't working on a financial level.

This was a flame that spread into an uncontrollable wildfire and sadly, it was driven by a handful of 'crusaders' who felt that they could do a better job than I was. Being a trail blazer and a pioneer who makes the journey easier for others comes with its downfalls and I would say that this was the biggest one.

Of course this high intensity caused me to lose sight of the fact that I had chosen to expand my business nationally at first and then internationally, to impact on children on a larger scale. With my business expansion came sacrifices. I had no time to coach children one on one anymore. I was working 10 - 12 hour days, 6 days a week, writing training programmes, developing products and fielding queries, but mostly doing admin.

I loved working with kids and I was supposed to be playing for a living, why then was my life spiralling into a corporate pit of despair? My franchisees seemed to think they owned me in more ways than one. They were all beautiful souls but highly dependent on the mothering behaviours I transferred to them as a result of being childless. I had made them dependent and reliant on me by always over delivering and this was part of my demise.

There is always a story behind the story that you may not yet know

I started blaming myself as a leader and chastised myself for letting my 'baby' go, and sharing my life's work with people who now didn't appreciate it. I became defensive and unapproachable and this was because of the fact that it felt like the people I had trusted to do good in the world were slowly chipping away at my dream.

My days became longer in hours and shorter in inspiration. In my mind my "job" was now to manage a group of people who couldn't manage themselves. With most of my franchisees being moms, I also became resentful that they used their children as an excuse that they were unable to spend time in their business. This was especially painful because I was unable to conceive children of my own.

Some of them were running their business as a convenience factor, wanting to follow their passion of working with other people's children, but at the same time using this as a means to spend time with their own children. There were, however, exceptions to the rule and in this wildfire of discontent, there were also loyal supporters, who were making their Kids Life Coaching businesses work.

It was confirmed for me then that in life, there are two types of people, those that complain and blame because they can't do it themselves, and those who get on with it regardless of the negative vibes surrounding them.

Look after yourself first and you can serve those around you more effectively

I gave my heart and soul to my franchisees, constantly trying to satisfy their needs, but knowing that some were playing me like a puppet. Coming from a teaching background, I was not a natural business person and had lots to learn but I was committed. I spent many hours educating myself on the ins and outs of business - attending courses, employing coaches and reading all that I could get my hands on.

All the while my mind was spiralling out of control. In my endless quest for meaning and due to my avoidance of dealing with my underlying personal issues, I made a few very poor investments, resulting in sinking myself financially.

One of these was very blindly setting up a school and investing all my hard earned savings into the renovations before I had officially purchased the property. I missed the deadline for raising my funding and the owner of the property stuck to his contract and took the building back without compensating me for the work I had done. This was despite my pleas for him to extend my time to secure a loan.

A hard lesson to learn, but it was one that I had to walk on my own, because so many people had advised me against the stupidity of spending money on a building before it was in my name.

Although it wasn't open, I had already successfully launched the school and had paid enrolments for the new school year, all of which I had to refund to parents. In business, some people are unscrupulous and I hope that the owner of that house who later went on to sell it as a school at an enormous profit, realise how wrong he was. The implications of sticking to our written contract for his own financial gain, when the finish line was so near for me showed his lack of integrity but also my naivety that business should be a gentleman's sport. That lesson I learnt is to tread more carefully and to realise that not everybody shares my values of honesty and integrity.

This coupled with a traumatic event related to some suppressed memories surfacing, ended up with me in hospital after threatening suicide to my husband. I stayed there for 10 days, drugged to the hilt and forced into a submissive lull in response to my burn out. Nobody except my husband and business partner knew, and that was the way I wanted it.

Others who knew me saw a relatively confident self-assured person full of life and love to give the world and I was determined not to tarnish this. My mask was intact and at that stage I intended to leave it that way.

On my discharge from the hospital, my psychiatrist had with much deliberation decided to attach the diagnosis of Bipolar to me. At the age of 35, he felt it fit to name my mental breakdown and classify me according to the highs and lows that had characterised my journey leading up to my mental demise.

Bipolar – which in the past was known as manic depression – is a severe mental illness that shows significant mood swings including manic highs and depressive lows. The majority of people with bipolar report experiencing alternating episodes of mania and depression. I had both, but I remember the gaps between these highs and lows shortening as my mind began crumbling.

For anybody with this illness, the symptoms can first occur and then reoccur when life's pressures are at their greatest. I was no different. Traumatic memories had resurfaced for me, and these "secrets I was unable to whisper out loud" were the catalyst for my demise.

For me, the key to coping with my Bipolar label was acceptance of my 'illness' and adapting my lifestyle, so that I was in control of the symptoms as much as possible. With the help of my psychiatrist, I was able to manage the illness with strategies involving medication, therapy and self-management that included terminating my dysfunctional relationship with alcohol.

Rebelling the system isn't always the best way

After leaving the hospital, I carried on working relentlessly on my return to reality, despite being heavily medicated. I managed to successfully put on the façade that I had been on a glorious holiday.

Although I didn't elaborate on where I was, I allowed people to assume that I had been lounging on a sunny beach rejuvenating my soul, when in fact I had been eating wobbly jelly and custard as standard hospital issue and wearing pajamas as my daily uniform.

Hiding the truth can be a lifesaver at times

I did escape from the sanitised hospital for a few hours once, near the end of my stay, but it wasn't a holiday. Not my proudest moment I will admit but another tick in my book of 'Bipolar' decisions.

Every day, whilst in hospital, I would go up to my psychiatrist's rooms in another wing, where he saw external day patients. During this time, he assessed my progress and provided much needed therapy. He was a passionate Italian, with a heart as big as the ocean, and he was kind and reassuring, yet he didn't compromise on his standards. He gave me strict instructions to get dressed in civilian attire for these appointments but I refused - having no desire to face the world with a facade of being fully functioning.

On the day that I did finally concede by adorning 'normal' clothes, he was running late due to an emergency. His receptionist, who was rude and obnoxious at the best of times, failed to inform me, so I decided to abscond in rebellion. I walked straight out of the hospital and went window shopping in a nearby mall, only to return a few hours later to a frantic husband playing detective with the hospital security team.

I can see how that must have traumatised him, considering I had been admitted to hospital after being suicidal, but at the time I had no rational thought. I can only deduce that the drugs I was on were one of the push factors for this behaviour.

For a year afterwards, I continued seeing my psychiatrist, who eventually turned out to be more of a friend than a doctor to me. Although I left each session with strict instructions to maintain my medication regime, he also reassured me that he had met many such people like me with the label of Bipolar who went on to live meaningful lives.

"Will I ever be able to stop my medication?", I asked him during one consultation. His answer was a resounding "No, not with your history." My biggest concern being on medication was that I was shaving off a decade of my lifespan. The drugs were potentially dangerous and the side effects, although not directly harmful in the short term, had been known to cause problems in long-term use.

"Would you rather be alive and happy now, or suicidal again?" Was his justification to me each time I asked him when I could stop my meds. Even with his discouragement I had already made up my mind that I wouldn't be a lifetime slave to these drugs. Another sign of the inner strength I gained through my extensive self-development work and my self-imposed research on brain physiology that underpins my Kids Life Coaching programmes.

Giving up comes easily when your heart was never really in the game

Sadly, after the short hospital stay that ultimately saved my life, my relationship with my business partner, started to crumble. She had always been a solid anchor to me, and despite the fact that we worked very effectively as a team, we decided to go our own separate ways.

She bailed when the going got tough, demanding a full return on her investment. Word got out about my inability to pay her back for her shares, as she disclosed the fact to numerous franchisees, who left with her shortly afterwards, claiming that the business would fold without her.

The irony was, that my once organised, caring, nurturing, stable, kind and unconditional business partner had become so absorbed in her financial bitterness and in telling her version of the truth, that she failed to see the repercussions of what she had done, and the contribution she had made to closing the doors of our business.

The difference between her and I was that I had no other option but to continue with my dream even if it meant doing it alone. For me there was no other alternative because I truly believed that I could change the system for children and that coaching was the way to do this.

The pressure became even more intense without my business partner around as she had helped with a lot of the administrative work. This forced me to make a hard but calculated decision that resulted in me dismantling all of the hard work I had done to build my business.

The payoff was momentary peace as I divorced myself from my "problem child" franchisees and relinquished their licence by voiding their original contracts. This risky decision gave them the rights to use my Kids Life Coaching programmes as they chose without legal repercussions.

It felt like I was putting up my 'business baby' for adoption with no recourse as to the level of the care it got but I did it with complete trust. Some continued my work under their own brand, passing off my intellectual property unethically as their own. Others returned to mainstream jobs, sacrificing their dream and family time to gain the financial upper hand again.

There were also some soldiers who stuck by my side despite the raging war that had hijacked me, when it would have been easier to buy into the group negativity and run. They were the ones that were committed to the bigger picture thinking that they shared with me. For them, it was about making a real and lasting difference in children's lives.

I am still in contact with a few of my ex franchisees and they continue to work with children in an authentic way with integrity and a heart filled with love. Sadly, this isn't true for the majority, with whom I have lost contact because they chose to buy into the stories about me which were unfounded and inaccurate. They judged me according to the behaviour that was caused by my mental health issues at the time.

Fitting in just to avoid being judged will eventually back fire

They should have known better, because when faced with my personal challenges prior to my mental breakdown, I was totally transparent as to the struggles I was facing. They are the status quo and the ones who above all else, value 'fitting in'. It is not easy to be an outlier and the one who does things differently. I am proud to still be amongst those that chose to walk the path of their truth because children were always and will always be at the core of their existence just like me.

There was, however, one true leader and pioneer who stood out above the rest, who remained fiercely loyal, and was a true testimony to living what she coached. My nickname for her is "Bokdrolletjie". This is a term used in the Afrikaans language that describes tiny round pebbles of deer poo, but it is a term of endearment that was given to her on a franchisee team building weekend away.

We went away annually as a franchise group and this particular time, our theme was "Build a child" and each franchisee was given a small handy man's toolbox filled with craft supplies and a hard hat to wear. My franchisees had been tasked to make a small gift for each other with a motivational quote using the supplies in the toolbox I had given them.

As an avid farm girl, born in the Kalahari, she collected Sheep "Doo Doo" as she called it and packaged it beautifully for us with an inspirational quote which I don't remember but it certainly brought on the laughs and made for a memorable occasion. This was one of the many times I saw the lightness in this beautiful soul and how she always interacted with integrity and authenticity.

Kalahari Bokdrolletjie was the only one who stuck by my side faithfully and continued to forge ahead with her destiny to empower kids despite what were perceived as my shortfalls. I feel honoured to have had this angel wrap her wings around me when I needed it most, picking me up when I was lost, through her unconditional belief in me. Her faith in me is what kept me going and was the antidote to all the negativity from those other franchisees that pulled me down.

She to this day continues to influence children in her community positively by using my programmes, and has launched multiple charitable projects, the biggest one being her annual retreat to the Kalahari where she invests her time into the Bushman families with a group of children each year. If I had children of my own, this is the lady I would want to coach them.

Taking a sabbatical from life can save you

After choosing to release my franchisees, "Kalahari Bokdrolletjie" included, and losing the essence of my business and along with it my dignity, I had the perception that I had tarnished my reputation. I thus quietly exited the Kids Life coaching industry and forced myself to go back to work.

Filling in job applications was the most heart wrenching exercise because to me it not only signalled the death of my legacy, but that I had failed the children. My dream to make a positive impact on children's lives globally was like Sleeping Beauty waiting to be rescued, and my confidence struck an all-time low.

Although I was well qualified and had a wealth of experience, being out of the mainstream job sector for so many years led to me being rejected for job after job without even gaining the foot in the door for an interview, oftentimes being told I was over qualified.

This disappointment and frustration which was exacerbated by financial pressure, made me succumb once again to the big "D" – the dangerous, dark, dismal, dreary depression a couple of years later. This led me to admitting myself voluntarily into a Psychiatric Health Clinic, after a consultation with my psychiatrist.

I knew that my suicidal ideation was a problem and luckily this second time around, I had the strength to do something about it before I fell apart properly.

In the privately owned hospital that was well respected and purported to offer high quality care in a holistic manner, I learnt yet another lesson that cemented my destiny.

I was on the frontline of experiencing what it was like to be treated as 'mentally ill' in an institution that was a temporary retreat for healing my heart and mind. I realised that despite my need for tender care and concern, I was just another troubled human on the conveyor belt that discharged patients after 21 days. I was simply a 'number' in a hospital file, attending a myriad of therapy groups which took place under a haze of medication.

When you lose your dignity you also lose your mind

It was here that I saw how patients very easily got nurses to incorrectly administer their Schedule V drugs as a double dose to them night after night. Not only did this show negligence and a loophole in the system when it came to tracking medication, but it opened my eyes to the easy access to drugs that some patients chose to trade for financial gain.

One of the most common black market trades being made on those hospital floors was Ritalin - a central nervous system stimulant - that was administered to many adult patients diagnosed with Attention Deficit Hyperactivity Disorder (ADHD.)

Stop trying to fix
what was never broken to begin with

In this hospital, I learnt that recreational Ritalin is crushed, snorted or injected and is fondly called by the street name "kiddie coke". This prompted me to research why, and I found that both cocaine and methylphenidate, which is the generic name for Ritalin, are stimulants that target the dopamine system. According to animal studies, Ritalin and cocaine act so much alike that they even compete for the same binding sites on neurons. A shocking thought when we think about how many children are being medicated this way.

My biggest jolt came though, when I first met the teenagers who were admitted to hospital alongside me. One girl was barely 14, with eye liner so thick that it matched the dark rings under her eyes - bearing witness to the fact that she had been addicted to drugs and alcohol since being a pre-teen.

"You got a light for me?", were the first words she uttered as she brandished a cigarette in her small hand. I was shocked at the way the teens were allowed to freely integrate with the adults. Not just any adults. Not the good role model types, who could influence them positively, but the types who were drug addicts, alcoholics and like me, weren't in a very good mental space.

Since I had never smoked a cigarette in my life, I replied with a rather dismissive, "Maybe now is a good time to quit." Not an ideal response, but given the fact that the hospital allowed her to smoke in designated areas usually frequented by adults who would not be a great influence, I didn't know what else to say at the time.

Worse yet, I wasn't really in a position to stop her. I could see her pain in those dark circled eyes, but I was so wrapped up in my own problems that I was unable to dispense my usual caring words reserved especially for young people like her.

This is a secret seldom whispered out loud. Adults tend to try and 'fix' children or tell them how to do things, when they themselves are making a mess of their own life. They are poor role models as a consequence, and children become confused by their behaviour. That is how I felt in that mental hospital. A place reserved for other people. Not people like me who were educated and knew everything there was to know about mental health.

After leaving the hospital, I put in a formal written complaint about the way the teens were permitted to interact freely with the mentally ill adult patients. In response, I was told that they were given base line rules to stay secluded and that there was always a chaperone on hand.

I never saw a chaperone and can only hope that things have changed. Their rules didn't stop these influenceable teens from fraternising with the more seasoned adults who had been admitted multiple times for heroin addictions and other such unsavoury behaviours that had the potential to be imprinted onto a child's mind forever.

One particular lady who was part of my therapy group was from a very wealthy family and she explained how she had been to the unit multiple times and that she felt her job was to take care of the younger kids so that they didn't end up like her.

The irony was that she had the mentality of a teen and her influence on these kids did nothing but fuel their desire to further rebel the system. Affluence seemed to be a commonality in the teenagers and many of the drug addicted adults. They were given too much money and too much freedom to do what they wanted with. This of course is generalised because I was in a private unit paid for by my medical insurance, so I have no doubt that the opposite is also true. Lower demographic teens and adults also become addicts but possibly their drugs of choice are cheaper on the pocket.

Being vulnerable doesn't mean you are weak

Whilst in hospital, I embraced the fact that I was broken and that I was ready to be healed but my heart bled for the teens who knew no better and seemed to see their stay simply as an unbearable punishment. I couldn't help but wonder how many of them would fall victim to their toxic lifestyles when they returned to the real world again.

I had a seasoned eye for seeing potential in children and even though my senses were dulled by the intense medication, I was able to discern that these teens were natural leaders. All they needed were the skills to channel their leadership traits into positive habits. Life Coaching is probably what they needed, but instead they got therapy. Lots of it that only served to fuel their belief that they were broken and undeserving of anything better.

It was here that I realised that there had to be a better way for these kids who had been taken out of school, confined to the sanitised hospital corridors and labelled as mentally ill.

One teen boy had visible self-harm scars littered across both of his arms that he wore like badges of honour amongst those dysfunctional adults, me being one of them at the time. In my opinion, putting young people in a mental facility has every possibility of causing a self-fulfilling prophecy that they could live up to in later life. Putting them into a psychiatric hospital because they had made drug induced or self-harm mistakes, or attempted suicide based on lack of guidance, peer pressure or high stress environments, to me, is no long-term solution.

Perhaps this is my ego talking, but I knew that I could add value to these kids more than the boring "lectures" as they were called did, as these "lectures" put little focus on how to practically deal with the real world. So much time was spent focusing on 'fixing' that in my opinion these kids had little chance of sustainable recovery when entering the real world. In fact, most of my own recovery was not linked to the fact that I was surrounded by a support team there. It was linked to my own attitude.

Sometimes ego is the voice that shouts the loudest when nobody wants to listen

I couldn't help but notice that the Occupational Therapist in particular who worked with both the adults and these teens was so incredibly young and inexperienced. As well intentioned as she was, she did really elementary work that would probably fade away as quick as it took the paint to dry on the works of art we were forced to create.

The purpose of occupational therapy can best be described by the professions' motto - that all individuals have a right to live life to its fullest. An occupational therapist can help people consider not only their needs, strengths, abilities, and interests, but also their physical, social, and cultural environment.

Why then was this not happening in that hospital? It got me thinking and I realised that perhaps her four year university degree didn't have enough practical life experience to go with it.

This was one of the reasons that I many years after this, made the decision to change my original franchise business model to a certification model. This has made my coaching programmes accessible to the masses who already have a good foundation in place, but need the practical application side from somebody like me who has the life experience.

There is always an escape route even when you feel the most trapped

Whilst in the hospital, I received word that I was short-listed for an interview at a leading global university, which gave me a much needed reprieve from being trapped inside my own head. When released from my 'healing holiday' as I bitterly liked to call it, I nailed the interview and I secured a part-time position lecturing Behavioural Studies.

I had previously lectured Bachelor of Education Students at the start of my part-time coaching career and so I knew I had the experience and I was looking forward to the new challenges the position would bring. Overnight, my enthusiasm and energy for life began to flow as I found new purpose, lecturing a diverse, multi-cultural group of talented students on a subject that I was not only passionate about but very well acquainted with.

I was also fortunate to be surrounded by colleagues who were like-minded professionals and who spoke my academic language. They were inspirational in their dedication to the students and I felt like I had found my new home. They were also highly intelligent with many of them completing their Doctorates and submitting their research diligently. I admired this and truthfully, I felt slightly out of my depth at times, even though I had previous teaching and lecturing experience that had paved the way for me easily integrating into this new university.

At the time I was no longer coaching children as I had lost my business premises where I used to work from, and along with it, my confidence. I also didn't feel that my new found label that was kept firmly attached to me with a myriad of medications, was conducive to getting results out of the children I coached.

I soon realised that in this education context I could make a massive contribution to the hundreds of students I was reaching on a weekly basis. A high percentage of my students would become parents in the future and a few were already, and I believed that they could benefit from my insights from a Kids Life Coaching perspective in amongst their official curriculum.

Hanging onto the last remains of my failed franchise, I used my coaching model and tools to inspire them to rise above their personal challenges, limiting beliefs and labels. My students worked hard for me and I worked hard for them in return.

We had a good thing going. I told them that if they worked with me, I could guarantee they would pass with a distinction. The operative word was "work" and although I drove them hard, their top class results were proof that with the right attitude the payoffs were enormous.

Everybody deserves a lucky break

Consequently, I received a letter of commendation for my unusually high number of distinctions received and was voted one of the most popular lecturers by the students themselves, who graded me with a score of 4,7 out of 5 overall in their formal evaluation.

The letter from the Vice Chancellor of this international university stated that: "Your unit results are superb, and reflect effort, creativity and skills. Your contribution is important because it has helped to contribute to a positive student experience for those lucky enough to participate in your unit."

If only he knew how those words boosted my confidence. I still have that letter neatly tucked away to remind me of how I came out at the other side after being admitted to hospital and how my 'fighting spirit' had allowed me to stay true to myself, but also at the same time to serve the students in my lecture room. All of this whilst on heavy medication for a mental health label they did not know about, and dealing with personal trauma.

Sometimes we are cursed with conditions out of our control

During this time, I was given a welcome reprieve to rethink my path and for that I am so grateful. I became a bit of a 'wall flower' and preferred to blend in rather than make waves, as I previously had done in other teaching positions. However this didn't stop me from being told off by my very astute boss at the time, for interfering in the affairs of two students who almost fell victim to trafficking. She gently reminded me that as qualified as I was, there were student counsellors available to assist and that I needed to stay within my job remit. She was right of course, but I couldn't help but feel like I wanted to do more for those two traumatised girls.

As a doer and go-getter and somebody not naturally inclined to give up, I started once again designing my ideal business blue print in-between preparing for lectures. I asked myself the age old and most commonly repeated question worldwide

"If I could wake up every day doing what I loved what would that be?" My answer came in three words: *"Educate, Motivate, Inspire."* I realised that this was vague, but ultimately it was this mantra that defined the evolution of my business idea, and it was through this that the seeds were planted that would later grow into my online school, The Kids Life Coach Academy.

With more clarity than I had had in a long time, because of my regulated medication, my husband and I decided to make a clean start to regain my mental freedom, away from the baggage and pressure of my crumbled life.

It felt like déjà vu as we were again packing our suitcases to leave our sunny South Africa like we had previously done when we first found out we couldn't have children in 2001. Moving back to London in 2014, was a gift cursed with conditions due to circumstances out of my control.

I was faced with obstacles that seemed insurmountable, but although I was being tested, I came to the realisation that I was being moulded for a greater purpose. It was at this time that I tried to convince myself that there was peace in the fact that although I would never be a mother of my own children, my destiny was to be a mother to millions of children that belonged to somebody else.

My thinking was that in London, I could give birth to a new me, but what it really ended up doing was show me that there was nothing wrong with the old me. It was actually just me overcompensating for not being a mom and nurturing a business that would never give me the job satisfaction of seeing a first step or hearing a first word.

I learnt through my business journey that there is actually no such thing as failure. Although I lost my franchise and a school, I see these as teachable moments that have equipped me with the skills I need to do it better the next time around.

I am not perfect and will continue to make mistakes. This is how we learn and we grow. I have heard some schools who have integrated the phrase "learning" and "failing" and refer to these growth opportunities as "flearning" to their students. I am a dedicated "flearner" in life but I don't let my past, or other peoples' opinions define my present or my future. I only let the lessons I have learnt shape my decisions for the better.

The Hidden Truths about failing:

- *Failure is an overused and overrated term that should be banned from the dictionary. There is no such thing when you embrace the learning opportunities life sends your way.*

- *Mistakes are simply stepping stones to bigger and better things if we choose to learn from them.*

- *Financial success in business is only guaranteed if your mind is in the right space. Your inner world is almost always a reflection of your outer world.*

- *Mental health is not spoken about because it is feared as unknown. Stigma is something that holds us back from being empathetic to others.*

- *It is often what happens behind closed doors that defines a person's actions. Don't judge them by what you cannot see, and always assume that there is something more to their behaviour.*

- *When you make yourself vulnerable and ask for help, there is always a way out. Nothing is ever too hard or too broken to fix with the right people on your team.*

- *There are always people in life who attempt to take what belongs to others and pass it off as their own. If this happens to you, see it as a compliment because you are considered a pioneer.*

- *Everybody has their own story. It is up to you to rewrite your ending if you need to, because your start never defines you permanently.*

- *Your past has shaped your current behaviour and it is only those who work on themselves that can break free from the prison of their own self-imposed limitations.*

- *Rebranding childhood is about taking the bad parts of your early start, and packaging them in such a way that you can move forward with positivity and strength.*

13

The GHOST IN THE FIREPLACE

Hidden Truth:
Adults don't always know the answers

Pacing, pacing and more pacing. He walked circles around me, not making eye contact. No visible signs of being aware of the world outside. Evidence only of being in his own bubble. A protective layer that wouldn't let me in. Sometimes his pace slowed down, other times it was so frantic that it left him out of breath and glistening with sweat. Only sometimes. It was in those sometimes days when he wasn't pacing, that I gained a snapshot of what it must have been like to live in a self-constructed dream world.

He loved to build lego and we had our best chats when he was constructing marvellous towers with complicated turrets and colour coded symmetrical patterns. On those 'sometimes' days, he sat with me chatting without a care in the world and very coherent. He was intelligent beyond his years for a 5-year old and articulate to the point of being adult like. His striking blue eyes framed an angelic face that was topped with a mop of unruly blonde hair and a beaming smile.

The label that was attached to his behaviour by his concerned and loving parents when we first met, was 'high functioning Autism'. At the time, I felt the urge to do a lot of reading up and researching, and the prognosis didn't seem to be that good in terms of coaching. With me though, there is always hope, so I knew something could shift positively even if it was only in a small measure.

His pacing, I soon learnt, was a coping mechanism to place order into his world when he felt out of control. It was an attempt at controlling those things that tried to control him and caused overwhelm in his neat orderly mind.

I very quickly became fully aware that when he paced with the most persistence, he needed me the most. It was on those days that he used this self-stimulated behaviour (which in proper terms is known as "stimming"), that he had faced something especially anxiety provoking.

I was just grateful that his choice of self-regulation was pacing and not of the self-injurious type that so many other children in the Autism spectrum participate in like head banging, or punching walls. Besides anxiety, Angel Eyes also stimmed to help himself to manage his fear, anger, excitement, anticipation, and a range of other strong emotions in between.

On the extreme side, Autistic children also do this to help themselves handle overwhelming sensory input such as too much light or heat or noise. Perhaps you have unknowingly stared at an Autistic child flapping their hands in public, flicking their fingers or rocking or uttering loud incoherent words? This is their way of coping with the sensory overload. Their behaviour is often met with disapproving and questioning stares because people are unaware of how clever their inbuilt self-soothing mechanisms actually are.

Perhaps you engage in nail biting or flicking your fingers or tapping your foot uncontrollably or you click your pen (you know the type I mean) annoyingly without repercussions from the people around you being irritated.

This is simply a milder form of self-soothing that all of us have used at one time or another to a certain degree. However, in Angel Eyes, his stimming was causing a breakdown in his world and this way of coping was not acceptable in the mainstream school he had found himself in.

On his parent's request, my job was to support him in finding alternative coping strategies that were more 'mainstream' and 'normal'. Just like your coping behaviour that you use in your stressful times to carefully blend into the masses and not draw attention to yourself. They wanted their son to integrate into society as an adult, fully functioning and emotionally regulated. Such marvellous foresight that so many parents of apparently "normal" children forget to gift them with.

You can't be pushed to the limits if you don't know what your limits are

Angel Eye's parents were a power couple with a string of successes behind their names. Young, attractive, affluent. Living in a large home fashionably decorated and looking like it belonged in the pages of a glossy magazine, framed by their big cars parked outside and going on luxurious holidays multiple times a year to exotic locations.

They worked hard in their respective professions but they played hard too, always doting on Angel Eyes and his baby brother. They were loving and involved, and two of the most caring parents I have ever met considering the challenges they faced.

In the time I got to know them, I watched them pushed to their limits multiple times, but they never gave up and to me that is true parenting. I admire parents who are pushed seemingly beyond tolerance but they still bounce back from the heartache and sleepless nights of worrying and seeking solutions. The essence of this is because they truly believe that the beautiful child they birthed should be and could be so much more.

Money was of no consequence to them and they had a myriad of professionals they consulted with, in search of the holy grail which was their son reaching his true potential.

After being asked to leave his mainstream school because he couldn't "fit in", due to his intense anger and violent outbursts, the parents had been forced to consider home schooling options. They chose only the best in the industry to support them, and Angel Eyes had already seen a multitude of top pediatricians, psychiatrists and educational psychologists by the time I was called upon.

I was handed reams of paper filled with repetitive medical terms and diagnoses but nothing concrete as an action plan for his future. Even I felt overwhelmed, although I was a teacher with years of experience in reading reports such as these, and held an Honours degree in Psychology of Education.

According to the professionals, the odds seemed stacked against Angel Eyes and the recommendations were vague and non-committal, leaving these proactive parents with no option but to explore other more concrete interventions.

Quirks should be celebrated
as a sign of individuality

Angel Eyes was a pleasant boy and from our very first initial meeting, he crept into my heart with such ease and grace, using his blue eyed charm to interact with me. That being said, I always receive children into my space with an open heart and mind and he could obviously feel this energy exchange as I interacted with him while his parents watched lovingly.

We played with his teddy bears and I couldn't help but notice that all of his other toys, which were in abundance, were highly educational. Mom and dad obviously paid a lot of attention to his development and these soft fluffy companions served to do little more than offer him comfort, but on that day, he chose to share them with me, a signal to me that solidified that I was chosen to be part of his inner circle. A compliment I valued highly from a child who wasn't able to accurately verbalise this need, not because of language deficiencies, but because the "touchy feely" bits were not something he was accustomed to.

It was an unusual first family consultation because unlike my other clients this took place in their home. This was where I would end up coaching Angel Eyes in a very unique position that I had been allocated through an agency specialising in special needs placements. I had just arrived in London and I was still building up my new business concept and so this was a perfect opportunity for me to not only gain a consistent income, but also to tackle a client unlike any other I had worked with.

My experience was solid and after interviewing me for this "home schooling" position, the parents chose me not because of my teaching background, but because of my coaching experience, as they saw this as additional asset. My primary objective in the year that was to follow was to reintegrate Angel Eyes into school again. He had developed an unhealthy aversion, and rightly so, because of the lack of tactful handling of his situation in his previous school.

My task would not be easy, but it was certainly one of the steepest and most rewarding learning curves that called upon not only my solid education as a special needs teacher but also my coaching experience. This boy was bright, and so although I spent time everyday establishing routines and doing numeracy and literacy, most of our hours were spent in play based learning that involved laying the foundation for the social skills he was so sorely missing.

Calming down is a skill that overrides irrational behaviour

Although he had outbursts that were tantrums usually displayed by a 3-year old, I had not seen the violence and aggression his parents had warned me of. Not until the day I caught a snapshot of this in his blue eyes that turned a startling dusky grey as he yelled the words, "I hate you. I hate you. I hate you."

These echoed through my head in reverberations the day he showed his volatile side. The screams eventually led to hitting, kicking, biting, pushing and pulling of my hair as he used me as his punching bag. Although I hid the fact from him, that I was very shaken after the first time this happened, I went home that day and cried.

It reminded me of my early days as a Special Needs teacher where the children were so filled with sadness, overwhelm and aggression that they often lashed out at me. Angel Eyes was different though and his didn't come from the same space because he was intelligent and displayed no learning difficulties other than controlling his emotions.

I had a deep empathy for him when he got like that. There were many such days to follow in our school year together and I had the bruises and scratches to prove it. Luckily no lasting damage was ever done except the time I ended up on crutches the day my mom landed in Heathrow airport for a visit, because I had chased after him and fallen down three steps. My torn ligaments have never healed properly and sometimes when my ankle aches in the cold weather, I am reminded of my days with him.

The pattern was always the same but my response started adjusting his reactions and soon he learnt that although his emotions were okay, expressing them in a violent way was unacceptable.

I created a "calming down" space for him with a cardboard box filled with all sorts of things to help him when he found himself in this state. Bits of coloured paper, polystyrene balls, bubble wrap, play dough, pegs, paper clips. In fact anything that I knew that would be a distraction and help him to channel his negative emotions was placed in that box. He loved using it and often I would spend more time picking up the pieces of finely shredded paper than it would take him to calm down.

I nailed his anxiety the day I realised that Angel Eyes was lonely. Children with Autism are sometimes pegged as loners who choose to keep to themselves but I soon learnt that with Angel Eyes this was not the case. He had a few friends but because of his strong willed personality, his play dates were always on his own terms. When he was in their midst, I was told by his nanny that he figuratively stood out shoulders taller than them as the leader, often to his detriment, because his forcefulness at getting his own way is what usually got him into trouble and ended up pushing his friends away. He didn't mean to, but isn't it true of many adults in power as well?

Look at those in positions of leadership who use their power to coerce others into meeting their own wills and desires. We see this in politicians and CEO's of companies, but their toys are their employees and followers, and their outcome is always profit or career advancement. They are no more than petulant children wanting to get their own way as leaders.

Every child is born a leader in their own right

I told Angel Eyes parents the first day we met that he was a leader and that I was keen to facilitate how he channeled that. I have no doubt that one day he will be in a powerful position. Possibly a rocket scientist? An engineer? A surgeon operating with intricate accuracy in a life threatening situation? A scientist finding a cure for cancer? An author destined to shape this world with his words?

Judging a child because of angry outbursts that led to him being excluded from mainstream school, like Angel Eyes was, is short sighted. I look forward to the day that our worldwide archaic education system spends more time channeling strengths and building life skills than trying to subdue children by putting them into a box.

I hope to see an evolving schooling system where children are encouraged to be leaders and they are not defined by the negative aspect of the label they may have been given, but by the aptitude they display when given the opportunity to shine!

It is a myth that people with autism don't want to socialise, I saw first-hand with Angel Eyes that he simply did not know *how* to socialise. The unspoken rules of social behaviour - the things that you and I and most other people use unconsciously - were mysteries to him. He was forthright to a fault and he often said things that got right to the point, and lacked empathy or concern for others' feelings.

Like the day he told me my hair was too curly and I should brush it more. Although my feelings weren't hurt, he did prompt me to tame the frizz by a much needed overdue trip to the hair salon!

Children choose to be authentic because they don't yet care that they may be judged for it

What I loved most about Angel Eyes was his propensity for telling the truth. He called a spade a spade and although this could get him into trouble, there is a lesson in there for many adults. We walk around shrouding our words in tactful half-truths, hoping to not hurt the people we are talking to. We end up compromising on our integrity and we fake our way through conversations only to get to the other side with a feeling of dismay because we haven't said all we wanted to. Children, and not just those with autism, have a deep sense of honesty that I respect.

When do we lose this as adults? When do we start modelling that it is okay to hide the real truth and that you have to sugar coat your words by saying the "right" thing just to please others or to avoid the possibility of getting into trouble?

I remember when my two nieces came to visit my husband and I on the farm, for a half term, and I first caught them lying to me. I never expected anything other than the truth and they were honest to a fault until they saw a threat of getting into trouble for losing my new gloves.

They then banded together like a pack of wolves, concocting stories fit for Pulitzer prizes! I saw them attempting to say and do anything to avoid feeling my wrath as an adult who may punish them for their child-like mistakes of being irresponsible. This is so typical of most children, who learn to lie because of the fear of repercussions and the discipline associated.

There is an implicit advantage for parents of autistic children. Unlike my nieces, who tried to sweet talk me out of their mistake of losing my borrowed gloves by concocting an elaborate story of how the sheep ate them, autistic children are terrible liars. They tell the truth every time and I see this as a distinct advantage in a world that is shrouded in half-truths and secrets whispered behind each other's backs only to be discovered later in a roundabout way.

I remember that look in my nieces' eyes the day I told them it takes more courage to tell the truth and face the consequences than it does to lie. That a true leader finds solutions to problems. That a true leader will never blame others but will take responsibility for their part. That a true leader doesn't lie to protect the lies of others. That a true leader will take the consequences when they make a mistake. That a true leader learns the hardest and most useful lessons when they make a mistake.

I explained that all leaders will eventually get something wrong. Even me....They understood, and that day I know I cemented their belief that they can tell me anything, anytime, no matter how badly they may have messed up. Our unspoken word was that no amount of messing up would stop me loving them, simply because I had authentically revealed that I myself have made massive amounts of mistakes and lying has never brought me reprieve.

Always tell a child the truth even if it is hard for you

I loved my morning routine with Angel Eyes and in fact, my mid-morning rice cake with peanut butter while he nibbled on his fruit became a welcome ritual for us. Children with autism rigidly adhere to a schedule. It becomes their anchor. If it's disrupted, they can become distraught. So I made sure day in and day out that he knew what we were doing, when we were doing it and what it would involve. I always met his expectations and never broke from my promises.

This simple act of consistence was one thing that his previous mainstream school had been unable to provide. It was simply him trying to adapt to a flexible and fluid school day that led to him lashing out at teachers and his class peers.

How I wish his teacher had taken the time to absorb herself into his intellectual obsessions rather than focus on the negative aspects of his behaviour which could have easily been channeled in other ways.

Another common autism symptom is an exhaustive and staggering knowledge of a particular subject. Angel Eyes was fascinated by the human body and space ships and historical stories of wars long gone. His thirst for knowledge was commendable and he often knew more than I did in many subjects simply because his parents had spent the time nurturing his intellect and nourishing his enquiring mind. Whenever I didn't know the answer to his questions, and he had many, I told him the truth that I didn't know and we would google it together during his Friday half hour of iPad choosing time.

Another simple truth that adults hide is when they don't know the answer to a question that a child asks. Many of them make up their own half-truth to appease the question by faking their way through the conversation. To what end? Surely telling a child the truth when you don't know the answer is more of a powerful lesson than giving them the incorrect information?

If you don't know the answer, say so. That way somebody can help you

As a teacher, I remember multiple times when I told children that I didn't know the answer. This made them aware that a teacher is not some demi-god who is all knowing and all seeing. In life, we have to admit when we don't know how to do something and stand on the shoulders of giants to find the answers when we need to. I loved finding answers with Angel Eyes, and his thirst for knowledge fuelled my desire to learn more and prepare better for our weekly themed discussions.

Circle time was our favourite bonding time and we spent countless hours seated on the plush carpet of his parents' formal lounge, expanding our circle of communication with his teddies seated alongside us as our fellow class mates. He often felt the loneliness associated with being home schooled for a year, and it was delightful to see him engaging with his myriad of teddies in different shapes and sizes during our special time at the beginning and the end of our 3 hours together.

I would always try to meet him at his developmental level during this time and build on his strengths. I would emphasise the value of our back-and-forth play interactions that established the foundation for our engagement and problem solving.

He was still young, so obviously he did lose concentration in this time, so I also helped him to maintain focus, to sharpen his interactions and to practice abstract, logical thinking, all essential skills in the school of life for one day sitting in a meeting irrespective of chosen career.

Play is the chosen
language of childhood

It was in this safe space that I saw him grow the most. It was with the use of my Zeal the Zebra puppets and my accompanying story book that I saw him push himself to his full potential. With my support, along with his parents, he developed into "who he was" rather than what his diagnosis said he should be. Just like my rainbow coloured Zeal the Zebra character, he was born to stand out and not fit in. At that stage, I had niggling doubts that he fitted the full profile of his autism label, but I didn't question it until much later.

Simply because I engaged at his level through play and allowed him to lead the activities, he started growing from the inside out and his parents and nanny noticed a difference. Family life became more streamlined and his relationship with his baby brother improved. This would later be reflected in one of the best testimonials that has ever been written for me, and I am still thankful for the opportunity the agency and the parents gave me to prove my worth in what were sometimes very challenging circumstances of my own.

What I was doing with Angel Eyes could be considered by some as play therapy, but in my coaching model I have taken the basic premise that play is the language of childhood and moulded it into a concrete way of opening the lines of communication. During our time spent together, I helped him to reach the developmental milestones that he needed for his emotional growth before he was able to reintegrate into school even though he hated it so much.

Our casual playtime allowed him to learn to have a healthy interest in other people and their world. With this "other people" being me, he found out what it meant to engage in meaningful human interaction where two-way communication is essential. He found out about my interests and he shared in my sadness on those days that I yearned to go back to my home country of South Africa.

It was especially on those days when the rain pelted down as an unrelenting reminder that England was to be my new life, that I disclosed my feelings to him. We engaged and problem solved and he would help me to find solutions to my BUG's (Big Ugly Grumpy's) which were the negative thoughts that brought my associated negative feelings.

Without the comfort of having my immediate family around me, I was a new born in a country that was different in every way than what I had been accustomed to. I defined my strong range of feelings to him with vocabulary that gave him the tools and the permission to verbalise his feelings as well.

He learnt to recognise when I felt sad through my body language and facial expressions and it was on those days that I got the tightest hugs and the highest high fives and the biggest of smiles. To me that was progress. Small progress, but hopefully it was this progress that would lay the foundation for his success in later life.

Real strength comes in showing up even when you don't want to

The calmness I exuded in my year with Angel Eyes was a stark contrast to the real secret I was hiding- that I was still on strong medication to control my own label of mental illness I had been given. I was, for the first time in over fifteen years of marriage, living apart from my husband. I was also essentially homeless, floating in-between other people's spare rooms as their guest, and for some, as a boarder paying rent.

I became accustomed to living out of a suitcase and saving as much money as possible to start a new life away from the financial burden of the mistakes I had made in South Africa. I was always treading around lightly with the people I stayed with, over compensating for feeling like I was in their way. I never felt relaxed or at ease, even when they tried their utmost to make things comfortable for me.

I had never been apart from my husband for any extended period longer than a few weeks, but in that year, I was living apart from him, not willingly, but because of circumstance as he finished his contract in South Africa before later joining me.

We had not planned this, but because of financial difficulties caused by my breakdown and other choices we had made, my husband and I were forced to take drastic measures.

I can only compare how I felt then to how I think a foster child may feel when placed in a new home. I felt so lonely, although I was supported by many around me. They went out of their way to distract me and make me feel part of their family but I personally never felt that I was.

There is an unwritten bond and rule that is never whispered out loud about family. Even with the closest of family and friends, their space is sacred, and as much as they have good intentions, their children and their life and their priorities always come first. As they should. As they do with my husband and I. It was just tricky feeling this and being an outsider looking in on happy lives when mine had fallen apart.

Home is where the heart is

In between my healing bruises from the physical abuse Angel Eyes inflicted on me in the first few months of my placement, he was also my beacon of light. He gave me purpose and clarity and quenched my thirst for doing more and being more. He planted the seed of doubt that I was truly the bipolar label that my psychiatrist had attached to me. Just like I was doubting my label, I was also doubting his, and it was at about the same time that I entered into a journey with his dad into questioning the diagnosis he had been given.

The exact cause of autism syndrome is not known, however, the fact that it tends to run in families suggests it may be inherited genetically. Many experts believe that the pattern of behaviour from which autism is diagnosed may not result from a single cause, and that some of them may be environmental. When Angel Eyes went for his observations and assessments, the doctors did an evaluation by performing a complete medical history and physical and neurological exam.

Many children with autism have low muscle tone or coordination issues and he underwent various tests to determine if there was another issue or physical disorder causing his symptoms. His pediatric neurologist and developmental-behavioural pediatrician eventually based their diagnosis on his level of development, and the observation of his speech and behaviour, including his ability to socialise with others. The doctors mostly sought input from his parents, teachers, and other adults who were familiar with him, and they simply categorised him as best as they could using the diagnostic criteria at their educated disposal.

On one particular day, an educational psychologist dropped in. She arrived as Angel Eyes and I were sitting down to eat our snacks. We had our routine, and she was an unwelcome break in this. True to form, he kicked off. Instead of stimming to self sooth as he usually did, he proceeded to lash out at me with words.

I welcomed this instead of the punches and bites I was previously used to being on the receiving end of. I remained calm and in control and continued to eat my snack, doing as much as possible to keep the routine similar as the very intrusive psychologist asked me questions about him in front of him.

Always speak as if a child is listening

This is something I have seen all too often in clients I have coached. Adults speak about children as if they are ghosts in the room. They ignore their presence and I am not sure if they truly believe their words fall on deaf ears or if they are just stupid. That in itself is a bug bear of mine and a debate that can be dedicated to a whole chapter.

For the purposes of this exercise, I want you to picture an overpaid psychologist who knows nothing other than what she has been told about this child. She had read the same reports as I had. She had a similar education as I had. Yet, she has the empathy of a rhino on heat! She barged into our space, our personal, nurturing space without proper introduction, without building rapport, and without any consideration for the feelings of Angel Eyes.

She appeared to be more interested in her upcoming ski trip, which she unprofessionally shared with me behind a whispered hand, than her job to be of service to that family who was paying her so handsomely.

A professional qualification does not entitle you to automatic respect

Why is it that some professionals who have studied for years, lack in the tact and decorum when they have made a name for themselves? Here is a secret I am going to whisper out loud. What gives a medical professional the right to treat a child with disdain just because they have a track record of results?

When does somebody become too good for themselves that they become delusional about the level of interaction with their patients or clients? All too often, it is these delusions of grandeur and their lack of emotion that bring them the results, but it does little to earn my respect, and simply put, I think parents, and more importantly, the children, deserve better.

In a world lacking in relationships and meaningful human connection, I still can't understand why this particular psychologist thought it appropriate to disclose to me that her visit was merely a formality in the final bid to make Angel Eyes autism label stick and get appropriate funding. She used the label in front of him as if he was a third party. A spare wheel. A citizen not worthy of attention.

No wonder then that he lashed out at me. I was supposed to protect him and he trusted me, so by letting this wild woman into our domain I was breaking my promise. This woman with her constricting conservative suit that screamed professionalism and matching stiletto heels that confirmed she was image conscious, with manicured nails and not a hair out of place, who thought she could impress me with her multitude of accolades and degrees and her expensive suit.

Yes I am judging here. I am saying it out loud. Forgive me if you will, but what professional who has chosen a career path dedicated to children wears a suit on their first introduction? Whilst I don't wear attire that children would dare to be seen in, I always dress for the occasion as this is a rapport building activity and my cool trainers or coloured T-shirt or my funky arm band is often a talking point with the kids I coach. It makes them feel comfortable and it bonds us on a different level.

If you want to get a child to trust you, you need to earn it. If clothing helps in this transition, I will wear a clown suit if I have to. If it means the child is left comfortable and at ease I will do whatever it takes. This is just one of the differences that makes coaching so different to the psychology field. I want to clarify however that I have met the most amazing psychologists who are masterful at building rapport with children and who embrace their job with the relevant decorum.

Building rapport with a child is simple if you respect their space and show them you care

In life, I have personally experienced that sometimes the greatest help is found by those who humble themselves and share the humanness of their personality. If I had been that psychologist and meeting Angel Eyes for the first time, I would have built a rapport by firstly apologising for intruding. I would ask him how I could fit in and make him feel in control of the situation.

Instead, as with some professionals, their power goes to their heads and they see little need for going down on one knee, making eye contact and speaking to a child at their level. Luckily, as I said, I have met many professionals who are the exact opposite of this psychologist, but she reminded me there is still lots of work to be done in the system to shift entrenched behaviours.

On that day, she reported back to me, "You did a really good job getting him out of the fireplace after his outburst. I thought it was touch and go but you handled it well." As if I needed her validation. As if she was doing me a favour by praising me for something she had created.

She claimed that her "cold" intrusion was a deliberate attempt to shift his routine to see if he would have an outburst. Have you ever heard such rubbish in your life? I had mentally prepared Angel Eyes for her visit and I knew there would be a break in routine, but what I hadn't prepared him for was her rudeness and lack of consideration and her inability to step out of her adult ego mode.

Any parent of a normal child who is hungry and in a routine would take great offence to a stranger who deliberately tries to trigger an emotional outburst in their child for their own agenda. This is why I am so distrustful of many reports written by some of the so called professionals who think they can classify a child as a textbook case. I always read these reports as they do add value, but I make my own judgements based on getting to know the child properly.

It is only in building a proper relationship that you can truly see the facts behind a child's behaviour. A one hour consult with a paediatrician or a visit to the psychiatrist who classifies a child according to the Psychiatrists' bible - The DSM (Diagnostic and Statistical Manual) - is not enough to conclusively attach a label to a child that could influence their future potential and possibilities in life.

At this stage I also wish to point out to anybody who sees a label as a way to gain help, treatment or funding to do so with much thought. Once that label is attached, it remains on record and will always be an "unwritten" thorn in your side if you at some stage choose to discard it.

There are many ways of looking at a problem

Angel Eye's dad pointed out to me after his extensive and most productive research, that he thought his son fell more into the category of PDA. This is an uncommon diagnosis that he thought was missed by the doctors. Through his reading and researching as an educated and interested dad, he found that Pathological Demand Avoidance is increasingly, but not universally, accepted as a behaviour profile that is seen in some children on the autism spectrum.

He concluded that the only time his family saw outbursts in his son was when they requested him to participate in everyday tasks that he wanted to avoid. When an adult placed their expectation onto him, he would do everything in his power to take control back. His resultant behaviour of hurting others or breaking things was deeply rooted in an anxiety based response of him needing to be in control.

The more I got to know Angel Eyes, the more I agreed with dad that he certainly did show a lot of traits of using social strategies such as distracting, making excuses, simply outright refusing, having mood swings, being impulsive or on the extreme end lashing out and hurting as part of his avoidance.

To the outsider, such as the rude psychologist, this behaviour would appear to be controlling and dominating, but to those that understood him, it was simply about giving him added support to make him feel secure and in control from inappropriate demanding.

Listen the unspoken story when resistance shows itself

Think about a particularly resistant child you have faced. When they decide they don't want to do something it becomes a power struggle, often ending up with the child crumpled up on the floor kicking and screaming or in tears. With Angel Eyes, we made this transition from "his child world" into "my adult world" a little smoother by mentally preparing him for any demands I would make. This is not a bad thing even for the more able child who is better at regulating their emotions.

Angel Eyes hated the library and in particular this was the one place he wanted to avoid at all costs. It reminded him of school and he hated school. So I made it our mission to go there together once a week. He told me he loved the books but he didn't like the people and especially the other children. He said it was too busy and he preferred being at home in his own library which consisted of a beautiful and impressive array of books that his parents had carefully and considerately purchased.

Knowing his need for control, I would mentally prepare him for this trip on a Thursday at home time by reminding him to read his library book from last week. Then I would ask him on my arrival the next day if he enjoyed his book last night and then I would once again share that we would be taking our trip to the library. I showed him on the clock when we would be leaving and explained what we would be doing leading up to that. Then when we were ready to go, I would ask him which shoes he wanted to wear and if he wanted his yellow raincoat in case it rained or if he felt his jumper was enough to stay warm.

This simple mental preparation gave him small incremental choices along the way leading up to the event so that he could still feel in control. I won't lie to you....I did have a gumboot or two thrown at me, and was hit with his umbrella once, but eventually this articulate mental preparation helped him to ease his anxiety.

Communication is about the subtle hidden truths in between that are better said out loud than avoided

As an outsider looking in, I can't help but wonder if parents communicate enough with their children. If they mentally prepare them for their breaks in routine. If they find the time to give them incremental choices that leave their children less anxious and more compliant.

When children are told what to do, there is a natural resistance to authority. I am an adult and although I was mostly a good girl, I have always had an inner struggle with authority. So I wonder if parents would benefit from a gentler approach at times.

In an ideal world, giving children choices all the time would lead to more spontaneous problem solving but I know that parenting sometimes leaves little room for the time to do these things. I can't help but wonder however, how many temper tantrums could be avoided if an adult stopped exerting their control of the child simply because they want to be the winner in the power struggle.

As an aunty, I love spending time with my nieces and nephew and I have minor power struggles with them. Usually these are related to safety, with no compromise ever happening when it comes to their physical well-being. That being said, I never make them feel like I see the world as such a dangerous place that they can't take calculated risks. I try to give them the impression that I trust them to make good choices for themselves.

Like the time my oldest niece refused to join me for a walk in the forest because she was scared of being stung by the nettles. She had fallen into a patch of nettles years earlier whilst riding her bike, so no wonder she was so fearful. I coached her to tackle the nettles as if she was a problem solver. To take calculated risks and to face her fear. I really didn't want her to get stung, but I mentally prepared her for the eventuality if she did get stung. She felt confident in the fact that the worst that could happen was that the sting would last for a few hours and that I had special spray to take away the worst of the burn.

In life, adults try to control kids through power struggles, scare tactics, fear and control. They are faced with endless rules that sometimes become fluid because a parent or teacher becomes too lazy or exhausted to follow through. They get confused. They make mistakes.

They don't have Pathological Demand Avoidance like Angel Eyes, they are simply children. They like to feel safe in a sometimes very confusing world where they are learning all the time. They are sensory beings who like to explore and if we inhibit this natural curiosity by placing too many expectations on them, they become anxious and fearful.

Adults are sometimes more needy and dependent than children

I was very proud of the day that Angel Eyes was reintegrated back into school. After a year of coaching where I worked on changing his story, his attitude to school was fresh and shiny and brand new and I was so pleased that he found a placement in a special needs school with dedicated staff who understood his needs.

I spent his first week in his new school with him but actually it was more for me and mostly for his parents that I did this. It turns out he was so excited about his new adventure and making friends that he told me on his second day there, "I don't need you anymore, Zelna. You can leave now."

This was not an insult, but the greatest of compliments as it showed me that he had regained his confidence. I knew that he would be happy in this school where his teacher was an expert in helping him navigate his sometimes scary emotions. There are many schools like this one that is skilled in accepting the child as they are and nurturing their strengths rather than trying to fix their "weaknesses".

The teachers that work there are my true heroes. The teachers who love the children in their classroom even when they know they may go home at the end of the day with a black eye or a bloody nose. They return the next day with even more love and an even wider smile and an even chirpier voice because they really, genuinely care. The real secret behind why Angel Eyes found his mojo back in school is that I genuinely believed that he would. He always had it in him, he just needed me to facilitate the process as his coach.

The Hidden truths about vulnerability:

- *When we show our real truth without fear of judgement, we often earn the most respect.*

- *Well-meaning people are still wrapped up in their own lives and even with the best of intentions their selfish needs get met before your own.*

- *All offers of help aren't worthy of acceptance. Only those who truly believe in a better outcome are worthy of being listened to.*

- *Don't buy into somebody else's prediction that is not based on all the facts. Stand up for what you believe in if it means enough to you.*

- *Children who are faced with unfair judgement will almost always build a wall around their heart to keep the adults who hurt them out.*

- *Adults who share their vulnerabilities with children willingly will always be remembered as authentic and stronger than those who try to pretend they have it all figured out.*

- *Lying is a self-protective way of avoiding the repercussions of disappointing somebody.*

- *True leaders face their problems with their head held high because they believe they can find a solution.*

- *It takes a village to raise a child and it is okay for parents to look to those who know more for their opinion. This however should never override their instinct for what is true.*

- *Vulnerability is that safe space that connects two people's hearts as one because they share a common denominator that serves others rather than expecting to receive.*

14

SECRETS WHISPERED OUT LOUD

Hidden Truth:
Speaking the truth sometimes comes with sacrifice

Many people say that everything is a choice, and I remember a lady once telling me to leave my husband and find a man who could give me babies. I want to clarify that I don't have children because I chose my husband instead. It is like the chicken and egg scenario. What came first? Well, my husband did, and perhaps I am old school, but I do believe love conquers all.

For me giving up on my marriage has never been an option. This has no doubt been passed down from my parents who have modelled this in their marriage that has stood the test of time and many challenges to come out okay at the other side.

My husband and I chose each other and ironically this turned out to be not only one of my biggest obstacles, but also my biggest gifts. Had I birthed children of my own, I may never have strived so hard to revive my dream to positively impact on children globally, after my first failed business. I believe that this was all part of God's bigger picture.

Despite this conviction, I have always perceived myself as an outsider who doesn't belong to any 'sisterhood of motherhood'. I will never be able to join in on the complaints of mothers speaking about their pregnancy war wounds of stretch marks on their belly or sagging breasts from having the life sucked out of them.

Over the years, my beliefs have become cemented by the fact that I have been left out of conversations about what the best brand of diaper is to not let poop seep out the sides, or the most eco-friendly washing powder that doesn't cause rashes. I have heard countless tales of mothers not giving the fathers of their children sex because they believe their role has shifted. Overall, I can say that through my experience I have been excluded from the perks of parent entitlement.

My perception is that some women who become mothers slip into selfish tendencies and they lose empathy for anybody who doesn't fit within their family realm. Unfortunately, it seems that this sometimes includes their husbands, who become outsiders in their own homes. I am not certain of this, but could this be one of the many reasons why divorce has become so common place? A mother is usually the one to choose her children over her marriage and as a result there is a high risk that may lead to broken vows made at the alter once upon a time when there were only two.

Parenting is based on survival

I once had a lively debate in Paris, with my dear friend, affectionately named as my "Feel good Fairy", who helped me to switch a light bulb on in my mind. She made me realise that mothers are instinctively territorial and that it is a primal survival mechanism to protect their young. This explained a lot to me about why so many mothers that I have met are so closed off to anybody that doesn't have the same life experience as them.

Neurologists have found that before a woman gives birth, there are changes in their brain and activity increases in the regions that control empathy, anxiety and social interaction. On a basic level, these changes are prompted by a flood of hormones during pregnancy and in the postpartum period, and they help attract a new mother to her baby.

In other words, those maternal feelings of overwhelming love, fierce protectiveness, and constant worry begin with reactions in the brain. Mapping the maternal brain has shown that there are several interconnected brain regions that help drive mothering behaviours and mood. Now here is an interesting snippet of information. Did you know that these brain changes aren't limited to new moms? Men show similar brain changes when they're deeply involved in caregiving.

The fact is that the blueprint for parenting behaviour exists in the brain even before a woman has children and I was no different. When I turned 43 something shifted in me and my mothering blueprint, still unsatisfied after 18 years of marriage, became severely unhinged.

Although I had managed to be at peace after years of therapy and lots of processing cruel remarks and being left out of the mix, the worst was not yet over. I suddenly realised as my doctor announced that I was possibly going through peri-menopause that my ovaries were gradually beginning to make less estrogen and that at some point they would stop releasing eggs.

The truth that I would never have morning sickness, or see my belly grow, or feel the kicks of a new life in my womb was debilitating. As much as I loved my husband and had chosen to walk the road with him, I developed an intense and inconsolable despair like none I had felt before. I started grieving for the child I would never have and I had no idea how to deal with it. Yet I silently convinced myself that I was okay mentally. The truth was that I wasn't okay and this wasn't the only reason.

Suffering from 'imposter syndrome' happens more often than you think

I had also been weaning myself off my anti-depressants and anti-psychotics for 18 months after convincing myself that my Psychiatrists diagnosis of bipolar 8 years previously was incorrect. I knew that I had experienced the manic highs and the debilitating lows, but I did not fit the profile in the true sense of the word. I had been diagnosed at a time of my life when I was faced with the loss of my business, the loss of motherhood, the loss of my home, the loss of financial freedom, the loss of family members. None of this was taken into account though, and unfortunately, although my doctor had good intentions, his diagnosis was one of the big reasons for the decline in my self-esteem.

Despite what I projected, I felt like a fraud being on medication, and spent numerous days curled up in bed wondering what would happen when my new associates, clients and friends I was making in England, actually learnt about the "real me".

I had a secret and I was ashamed. I was convinced that if people knew the real truth, they would judge me. It turns out I was correct about that in a few instances. I have experienced first-hand, the incriminating judgement and condescending treatment of those that I did choose to tell. Not all, but some.

Generally it was those with a heightened self-awareness and insight into mental health issues that understood and didn't judge me, but those who were uninformed did little to shift my unease with regards to sharing the secret plight of my mental health issues.

When I was invited to present a paper on my Kids Life coaching model at a Child and Educational Psychology conference in London, I was met with two schools of thought. Being one of the few non practicing psychologists there, I was met with fascination as I shed light onto the simple techniques I had been using to help children re-engineer their lives.

My proven model was substantiated by my lifestyle assessment that had a proven track record and after my presentation, I had many child psychologists congratulate me and reach out to me offering to help in any way they could. I even had those who said they had lost faith in the system they operated in and that my case for coaching was hopeful.

However it was one particular psychologist, well known in prominent leadership circles, who crushed my spirit with what appeared to be malicious intent. As a professional, she should have known better, but her behaviour is a clear illustration of how even in the most unexpected places, we find discrimination when we whisper our secrets out loud.

I was standing in the foyer of the immaculate hotel where the conference was held, speaking to a young, friendly psychologist who was enthusiastically sharing her insights into her latest research project. Mid-stream in our discussion, the malicious senior psychologist tapped me on the shoulder and looking me straight in the eyes, pronouncing, "Have you tried talk therapy yet? It seems like you need it because you were projecting your issues through your presentation earlier."

The look on the young psychologist's face was nothing short of embarrassment and my cheeks flushed with her in unison. In that moment, I was taken right back to my hospital stays, when I was first given my bipolar label after being suicidal. She had used this as my weak spot because I wasn't one of her "clan". I didn't fit the therapy gambit and I can only deduce that I made her feel uncomfortable since a lot of what I said was the truth often discarded conveniently by therapists because they refuse to accept there could be another way of doing things.

I believe in connecting with my audience no matter who I am speaking to, and sharing a personal story usually does the trick. So in my presentation, I had shared about my own mental health label and for whatever reason she felt it necessary to dispense her unsolicited advice inappropriately. Perhaps I would have received her advice better had she been more tactful, but in a busy hotel lobby whilst speaking to a colleague? I can't help but think at that moment in time, the irony was that she was projecting her issues onto me.

Our hidden truths keep us intact until we are ready to reveal the truth

The hidden truths we hold in our hearts and minds are often tucked away there to preserve our dignity and I can confirm that her attempt to humiliate me in public led me to carefully pick who I told about my label in the future. Although I now know that my secret is out in the open, I still fear judgment. Yet, I know that by speaking my truth, I could be the catalyst for others doing the same about their mental health.

The hidden truth is that we are the truth. Us adults who are meant to care for children and be good role models, tend to walk around with masks on. We project a perfectly made up version of ourselves to the world in an attempt to be liked and accepted.

What a beautiful gift we can give children by giving them insight into the fact that not everybody will be part of their tribe. It is up to you to choose who you surround yourself with and not the other way around. This is one of the reasons that I screen the Kids Life Coaches who join my global team.

I choose to work with highly passionate and articulate people who love children and see potential in even the most helpless of cases, just as much as I do. I could have grown my business quicker the second time around by being more commercially orientated, but for me values underpin everything that I do, my highest value being building solid relationships based on being authentic and speaking your personal truth.

A fraudster with good intentions is sometimes a necessary evil

On 2 June 2017, the day we started our new English rural country life, I declared proudly to my husband that I was officially drug free. I had romanticised the moment for months and had timed it perfectly to correlate with our house move from the vibrantly busy London I loved so much, to a beautiful rural farm blanketed in calm and bird song.

In my mind my new 'simple' life without medication was to begin in this beautiful space, and for the first time in years I felt like things would be different. It wasn't.

For starters, my husband was unimpressed that I had gone off medication without his knowledge. Despite my reassurance that I had done this responsibly with my doctor's support for well over a year, he couldn't shake the feeling that I might have been hasty.

Perhaps his intuition was right, because the 6 months to follow were a living hell of withdrawals and mood swings that threatened my marriage, further destroyed my confidence and left me spending endless days in bed.

What I didn't prepare myself for was for the fact that as my senses returned I started feeling again. I had been on medication for so long that I had forgotten what it was like to own my emotions and feel what a human being should feel. I also remember my skin becoming so sensitive to touch but in a good way.

I never once tied the fact that I had been on medication to my change in personality. My apparent lack of empathy. My inability to feel emotions deeply and fully. In the past, I had simply been placing a "band aid" in the form of pills onto my wounds every morning and evening thinking that this was how it was supposed to be. That this was better than ending up dead through suicide.

The first thing that challenged me when I stopped my medication was my yearning for alcohol. The past time of enjoying a glass of wine over a good meal and conversation had been one of my favourite social occasions. I used to be your classic "life of the party" girl, the one who didn't stop at just that one glass and ended up drinking the whole bottle.

In my drinking days, I was always the one to get the party going and then I would be the last one to leave. I was what one could class as a social alcoholic. I didn't drink during the week, and never alone, but at a social event and on weekends, I couldn't help but get recklessly drunk.

I had even developed a reputation for being able to maintain my alcohol and I was known by many of our friends as the Shooter Queen. I have many stories of handling my alcohol better than some of my husband's male friends who were seasoned drinkers. Usually ending in me hugging the toilet bowl and nursing a hangover for days after, but I still maintained my alcohol better than many men twice my size.

At the same time as my full senses started to return, and my alcohol cravings kicked in, my new business model of training and certifying Kids Life Coaches online through my Kids Life Coach Academy School started taking off.

I ethically and organically grew my team while I underwent immense transitions in my body, heart and mind because I was no longer on drugs. Yet at no stage during my long mental illness, had I stopped to acknowledge that I hadn't yet mourned and actually felt the grief of the loss of motherhood.

Learn to read the signals in your body before it is too late

This reality was harsher than I ever imagined, because think about it. How does one share with your inner circle that you are in mourning but you haven't physically had a funeral to attend? Nobody had actually died. The truth is that many of us mourn the loss of hope and we mourn disappointments. Just like losing a loved one, the grief cycle is the same. It just isn't spoken about because it is not as tangible.

The good thing about being admitted to a psychiatric ward twice, is learning to understand the signals in my own body and knowing what to do before spiralling out of control. In October 2017, a turning point came for me.

As my body finally rid itself of the final remnants of medication, I became suicidal again but this time it was different. As I sunk into the deepest, darkest depression, I knew that the voices in my head were untrue. I managed to erase the script that told me I was worthless, a fraud, a waste of air. In amongst my long hours of sleeping in a darkened room as the sun shone outside, I managed to speak some sense into myself and with much counselling from my husband and my close inner circle of supporters, I made a very responsible decision.

Sometimes you need to give yourself permission to 'drop the ball'

I bravely announced to my small global Kids Life Coaching team that I needed time out because my mental health was suffering. I told them my aim was to focus on being creative and finishing this book that you are reading right now, as that fed my soul.

So I did what any author does and I set goals and deadlines related to my big dream of publishing this book, because I believed it would change the way people think about Kids Life Coaching and contribute to making it mainstream. Yet, even with time on my hands I couldn't gain momentum. I couldn't understand why it wasn't happening? I believe it was because God had other plans for me. His plan was for me to heal and rest! I knew this, but I love writing, and at the time, I believed writing was resting, yet I couldn't even bring myself to put words to paper.

Despite deciding to rest for the tail end of 2017, I did run two live trainings without falling apart at the seams. I remember feeling euphoric during my moments of what is commonly termed as "being in the zone." I love teaching, and being around people is tonic for my soul, so when my business coach and close friend at the time recommended I go ahead with my previously allocated training dates, even though I was feeling dismal, I didn't hesitate.

He himself had been diagnosed with a brain tumour and was fighting the good fight and he inspired me to step up and put my best foot forward. He never complained, showed fear or fell into victim mode with his illness so how could I possibly use my depression as an excuse? His belief in me was a tonic for my weary soul. I still don't know how I pulled it off, but it wasn't the first time that I had put on my mask and hidden the truth about my depression to those that didn't know my real secret.

What I didn't realise is that I had lots of internal struggles that I had been suppressing for so long. Like finally acknowledging that it was necessary for me to mourn the fact that I will never give birth to my own child. Like overcoming a mental health label that held me back for years.

During this time off from life, I cried. I hid. I hurt. I got angry. I allowed the pain to consume me. It overwhelmed me. It overwhelmed my husband who didn't know what to do with me. Yet, during this time I was gentle with myself and gave myself permission to "drop the ball" while I wallowed in my own self-pity.

Luckily I had managed to surround myself with a small team of encouragers and fed my soul with the indulgence of just "being". I abandoned my to-do lists. Kept appointments to a minimum. My days were swallowed into the bliss of no structure.
I just fed my chickens. Read books. Watched movies. Listened to podcasts. Went for walks. Ate too much cake. That last part is the absolute truth. I really did eat too much cake and chocolate, and the reason is linked to science.

Self-preservation comes in many forms

We are born hardwired to like things that taste sweet as a survival mechanism to protect us from eating toxic foods. This is why if you're feeling stressed out, anxious or depressed, you may crave sweets, cakes or desserts and find that they make you feel better, even if only temporarily.

There is a complicated relationship between sugar, your brain and mental health. Very often, the dysfunctional side of this starts in childhood, with an abundance of access to highly processed, sugary foods and fizzy drinks. Parents who aren't aware of, and checking sugar content in common place food items like cereals or yoghurt, are doing their children a disservice.

What we need to understand is that the hidden truth is that cancer loves sugar. So do diabetes, heart disease, ADHD (Attention

Deficit Hyperactivity Disorder) and an A to Z list of other diseases and disorders. Yet for some reason, many parents are in denial and continue to overdose their children with too much sugar on a daily basis.

When coaching children, one of the first things I recommend to them if they are addicted to sugar is to reach for water instead. A tell-tale sign of a sugar addiction is noticing what a child does when they are thirsty. Do they ask for water or something sugary like fruit juice, soda or flavoured milk?

Sugar is a very addictive substance and children develop cravings for this at a very early age. I know when a child is not addicted to sugar because they typically ask for water when they are thirsty. Test the theory and see if this small simple truth is evident. I can guarantee that a child who reaches for fizzy drinks instead, is quenching their sugar craving before their thirst.

Over my years as a self-reformed chocolate addict, I have realised that there is still a time and place for sugar. In fact, I love sweet things. Probably because I developed a propensity for this in childhood. For me this is now linked to choice relating to the taste satisfaction, whilst in the past, it was usually linked to easing my low mood. At the time of my meltdown I can see why I turned back to that comfort, but I controlled it and didn't let it control me like in the past.

The truth is that in many children, their bodies have built up such a high tolerance for sugary junk food that their behaviour doesn't even change. You can compare sugar to kids, to what alcohol can be to adults. There are adults who get drunk after one sip of alcohol, and other adults who are regular drinkers like I was, with a high tolerance.

If a child drinks a can of cola and you don't see a behavioural change, this is a big sign that they are consuming too much sugar. I have also seen the opposite extreme of many parents who completely abolish all sugar from their children's diets. This leads to other complications like a complete intolerance to sugar so that when they do partake in the occasional treat, it can end in disaster.

Be kind to yourself because the world deserves to see the best of you

During my sabbatical from life, I gave myself permission to let go and release my pain. Through actually feeling and processing my emotions, it was like a light bulb went on. Luckily I was safely cocooned in my little island of rural farm land and can only liken my emergence, whole and restored to me undergoing a cathartic metamorphosis into a butterfly.

A lot of this can also be contributed to the fact that for the first time since moving to England, we had a small support network around us in the form of willing and kind neighbours. Their unconditional acceptance of us into their little community happened from the outset and was a tonic for our weary souls that had gotten used to doing things on our own.

Simply by giving myself permission to stop driving so hard towards my big goals to support children, I was able to give myself the space to heal. In this time, I nurtured new friendships not only with others, but most importantly with myself.

Taking time to work on myself has given me the energy to share the best parts of me with those who are interested. I need to disclose that I am making this sound easier than it actually was. The road was long and hard and treacherous and along the way, I have lost friends, offended loved ones and denied the hidden truths.

I still have secrets. Some things that are stored in the deep dark recesses of my mind, but I have learnt to tuck them safely away because I don't need them anymore. They were once part of my reality, but they no longer serve me and they certainly don't define me. I don't feel the need to talk about them, because it only brings me renewed shame or discomfort or pain. So I have blocked them out and my refusal to succumb to the lure of remembering them, is my coping mechanism. I have chosen this over choosing a life of victimhood which for some, is an easier alternative.

Some secrets are not meant to be whispered out loud

My real story is not written in the pages of this book. It is safely stored away in the filing system of my brain, where nobody can access it unless I choose to give them a pass. You may have met the person who is constantly telling the story of being a victim over and over, as if it gives them permission to behave negatively or make bad choices. I don't want to be one of those people. Our life is in our hands just like our children's lives are in our hands.

For me, it wasn't always like this. There was a time when I didn't know that my deep dark secrets even existed. They were stored safely by my unconscious mind only to resurface one day when I was able and ready to process the pain. For most of my adult life, they were totally hidden from my daily awareness, yet they dramatically affected my everyday behaviour and emotions.

Many people don't realise that hidden memories that can't be consciously accessed usually protect us from the emotional pain of recalling a past event. Without us knowing what this event is, eventually those suppressed memories can cause debilitating psychological problems, which in my case were over achievement, anxiety, depression and on the extreme side almost giving in to suicide.

Secrets can trap us in a cycle of despair

Just like I have secrets and you have secrets, every family also has secrets, those deep dark hidden truths that are shrouded in amongst their smiles and pretences that all is okay on the surface. For some, these are small irrelevant truths that wouldn't make much difference even if the world knew. They hide their secret in an attempt to preserve their dignity and to ensure ongoing respect. To save face.

Their secrets are the cohesion that keeps them loyal to each other as a family with love at the core. United in that one thing that the world doesn't need to know and the binding glue that holds them together. All families have these intimate secrets that are best left unspoken.

Then there are those families that have bigger secrets. The ones that risk them losing the world as they once knew it if anybody found out. They know that if that secret was revealed, it would change their lives forever. Their secret goes against the mainstream accepted norms and in so doing, it defies all logic. The hidden truth may sometimes be evident to those on the outside looking in, but there is often not enough proof. So everybody just carries on as normal.

In amongst these secrets, these lies and hidden truths, are children. The innocent, who are raised to not speak their own truth as adults. They are shown by the broken and damaged adults that are supposed to care for them, that it is okay to hide vulnerabilities and mask mistakes. Through this they learn the unwritten rule that to be accepted, you need to be perfect. They get the message that being 'different' and asking for help is not okay. This unspoken pact between parent and child sometimes has the potential to change their lifetime trajectory and not always for the best.

For some children, their deceit may be in protecting the ugly truth of dad arriving home drunk each night and beating up their mother. It could be a milder version of parental fighting leading to eventual divorce. Or they may preserve mom's dignity as she lies in a dark bedroom, nursing her debilitating depression. Some learn at a young age that money problems deserve to be hidden. That being poor is not acceptable. Or they hide the truth that their parents spend more time with their work colleagues than with their family. In my experience as a Kids Life Coach, this kind of neglect is visible to the trained eye, but just obscure enough to avoid any real finger pointing.

Then there are those children who are the actual secret. They are victims of abuse, whether physical, sexual, emotional or psychological. Their role is to accept the pain, to feel the confusion, and to succumb to the adult threats that should they tell anybody, the consequences would be dire.

For them holding this secret in the inner most chambers of their heart is what ends up potentially destroying them as an adult. It is up to us as adults to be on the lookout for signs of this in the children we care for. This doesn't mean becoming overly anxious, what it does mean is educating children on their rights to protect their body, heart and mind from abuse and what to do should they fall victim.

The only constant we can fully rely on is ourselves

Every journey has twists and turns that can either sink you or force you to swim. I sunk many times, but I am still swimming, and the only reason is because I can safely say that I have spent time building a new me. My personal brand has shifted dramatically from the ego-fuelled early days in my first failed business, and I now drive my decisions based on what is in my heart and not in my head.

The only constant that we can all have is to work on ourselves as adults because I believe that when we are happy, this will overflow and spill into children's lives. The hidden truth behind all of the childhood stress, anxiety, depression, self-harm and attempted suicide we are seeing can be summed up in one word and that is 'confusion'.

The world is a pressure cooker with a mismatch of conflicting ingredients that is cooking up a concoction of side effects. There is a plethora of evidence that is permeated with truths, but also filled with perceptions that childhood is changing, and indeed it is, but we need not stand helplessly by and do nothing.

Just like my trying journey of pain, shame, hard truths and almost losing my life to the voice inside my head, I know that there are people who might not make it like I did. There are those stragglers who are making mistakes and who might possibly never recover.

This is why we need to claim our own personal story and use it to our advantage. I have no shyness in proclaiming to the tweens that I coach that I used to line up ten tequilas on the bar counter when out partying in my student days. You see, my experience makes me a tour guide that can hold their hand and warn them of the pitfalls, but still give them enough space to make their own mistakes so that they can learn.

So many parents and adults in general, feel the need to correct and discipline children, yet they aren't running their own lives with any real conviction. For example, why can't a teen smoke if their parent smokes? Is it an age thing or a health thing? Why is it that we have a double edged sword when it comes to children where every move is watched and modified, but adults get to make decisions lacking in accountability just because they don't need to officially explain themselves to anybody?

Don't tell children what to do, rather show them how it is done

I'd like to believe that this book has given you the inside track on what I perceive to be what many parents may experience as they raise their kids. Unfortunately I have seen some parents who do give up eventually. I have never understood the parents who reject their children who confess their truth at being gay. Or the parent who has bailed their child out of jail multiple times and eventually cannot bring themselves to do it again. Or the parent who is abused and assaulted by their own child, because of drug or alcohol abuse. So much in our broken world can be prevented if parents just tap into their unwritten, unspoken promise of being a good parent to their child no matter the mistakes they make.

Many parents that I have worked with ask me why their children listen to me but when they ask their child to do the same thing, they are ignored. The truth is simple. If you want to get through to a child, don't tell them, show them. Being a role model is about sharing unconditional, unconventional, upbeat, upliftment that inspires them to make good choices.

When children are not given the ability to make their own decisions and they are constantly told what to do, they will eventually end up resisting. So the secret is simple, as a Kids Life Coach, I tap into my own inner child based on the fact that to relate to children requires me to speak in a language they will understand.

The language of childhood is play. There is however a fine line between acting child-like and being childish, and many adults fail to understand that boundaries are essential in adult-child relationships. Children are not looking for adult friends to overcompensate the fun factor, they are looking for adults who support them and understand what it means to make mistakes themselves.

Parenting doesn't have to be a lonely journey. There are many Secret Parents who really care

So what kind of adult are you really? Are you responsible, care free or somewhere in-between? Embracing your own inner child is the key to getting through to children. What it means is taking the much needed time to heal your past hurts and to choose the learning opportunities from those things that were sent your way to test you and help you grow.

It is about rebranding your childhood because in each of us, there is a young child who may have had times of difficulty or trauma growing up. None of us are an exception to that rule. As well-meaning and good intentioned as our parents were, somewhere along the line, they were unable to protect us from life knocking us down. This is the truth that we cannot bear to say out loud, but in essence it is only when children are really tested with their own trials that they have the potential to grow into the best versions of themselves.

I think parenting is the hardest job in the world and it is so easy to mess up if nobody tells you the 'unwritten' rules. The thing is it all starts with being an adult who takes care of their own mental well-being first, and chooses to be a role model that is worthy of looking up to, however this growth cannot be done without positive support and intervention, so never be afraid to admit you could benefit from help.

I believe that Kids Life Coaching is the way around children incorrectly processing life events that need not lead them onto a path of poor choices because they were lacking in support. Almost every single person I have trained as a certified Kids Life Coach tells me that they wish they had the opportunity to have a coach when they were younger. Many had good parents like mine, who gave them immense love and support, yet they felt that they would have liked an objective adult to share their everyday challenges with.

I always explain it like this to parents. Most of them have life insurance, car insurance or home insurance. This is for in the event that something goes wrong. The policies are in place simply for peace of mind. Kids Life Coaching is exactly like that, and if children are coached before the age of 12, it can give parents the reassurance and peace of mind that no matter what happens, their child will be okay. You see, it isn't in the daily events when parents are present that we need to worry about. It is in those times when parents aren't around that children are forced to make choices based on what is in their heart and not their mind.

Values underpin all choices, whether good or bad

A good solid set of values are the key to nurturing a mindset that embraces challenges with confidence. Whether you choose to base these on theological or spiritual principles or not, life is about a series of choices based on our own internal moral compass. Every choice we make has the ability to have a positive or negative impact on our own or somebody else's life. All of these choices are made based on our five basic needs of: survival, belonging, power, fun and most importantly freedom.

The process of healing your wounded inner child is one that involves navigating grief and embracing the feelings of shock, anger, sadness, remorse and loneliness. For your wounded inner child to come out of hiding, they must be able to trust that you will be there for them in a supportive and non-shaming way.

I believe that there is no such thing as a bad parent. I just see parents who make bad choices because they are still operating from a space of being a wounded child themselves. Anything they did to wound their children, whether done out of ignorance, neglect, malice or sheer defiance, does not define a child for life.

Just like so many famous icons in history have managed to overcome their early years of adversity, so can any child. Although their brains are potentially wired differently and like me, through their early trauma can be susceptible to mental health problems, there is always hope.

I used my own coaching model that I share with children, on myself. Through using my own tools, I have managed to successfully remove my mental health label and function medication free when once this wasn't even an option. I am also more articulate in my goals, my confidence has soared and my true purpose is now a reality.

It is all about rebranding your childhood because in each of us, there is a young child who still wants to come out and play. This is the hidden secret that will save our future generation from unnecessary pain, self-destruction and possibly years of unnecessary therapy. Every single parent, with all the good intentions in the world, will at one stage or another do something to their children that they regret. It is what they do after their mistakes that counts and can be the pathway to their child's emotional, social and intellectual freedom in years to come.

Your truth can make or break you but you get to decide

So what is your truth? What is your secret that you need to whisper out loud? If you need to, make a decision to tell somebody and get help. If not, tuck it away neatly in the dark recesses of your mind after dealing with it and choose to not let it define you any longer.

If you want to stay well in body, heart and mind then be sure to stay true to yourself. There is no use in faking it till you make it. Show the world your war wounds and life scars....this doesn't make you weak, it simply makes you human.

We need more people to feel comfortable speaking up about the state of their mental health and that is why I hope that you will take action in helping a child to rebrand their childhood into the lasting memories they deserve to have.

This is the essence and the beauty of Kids Life Coaching which can forever change the pathway of a child's life simply because they have a toolkit for making better choices based on what is real and true and right in their world. Not what we have been led to believe through social conditioning.

Abandoning the formal structures of archaic thought processes is the only way forward. We need to raise children to question those "Secrets that need to be whispered out loud" with dignity and not just to accept things blindly. We need to encourage children to find their strengths and utilise them for the good of mankind. It is only in serving humanity with what is good and whole within us, that we can truly change our world for the better. It all starts with us as adults.

Hidden truths about childhood:

- *Children have a hard time navigating life. There is so much thrown at them and very seldom do they have anybody to help them process this.*

- *Kids Life Coaching is a remedy for the problems we are seeing in childhood. This non-invasive method can be used by any adult who has been a child.*

- *There is an inner child wanting to come out and play in every adult. Have the courage to allow this to happen and you will flourish.*

- *Parents aren't necessarily bad if they are simply repeating the patterns they learnt in their childhood. If nobody has ever shown you another way, how can you be judged for it?*

- *Sugar is the one of the biggest hidden evils in childhood. It is destroying our children's ability to concentrate, think and learn.*

- *Every child deserves to be respected, nurtured and raised in a loving household. When this doesn't happen, there is still hope. There is always hope when a neutral external adult steps in and helps.*

- *Every adult is perfectly positioned to be a good role model to children simply because they were children once and know how hard it can be.*

- *Children should be allowed to question the incongruence in behaviour that some adults display. Their healthy curiosity into why there are different rules for children and adults may raise awareness and bring about change*

- *It is no longer acceptable to raise children according to outdated ways of thinking and doing things. There is too much information available to plead ignorance.*

- *Children are tougher than we think. Just because life throws them curve balls that may be hard or challenging, doesn't mean they won't be a success in life.*

Epilogue

What can I do now?

I have seen first-hand what a negative mental health label can do. I believe that I was never "crazy" or "bipolar". I was just broken from a series of traumatic experiences that left me emotionally and physically burnt out. I hid it from the world, but it didn't do me any good because my self-esteem was impacted, and I was left feeling deflated and unworthy. I lost my dignity, identity and my will to live, and I allowed it to define me when I was at my most vulnerable.

I had all the skills I needed to overcome this as a scholar of all things "self-development", yet even I wasn't able to lift myself from the deep dark depression caused by a myriad of life events that were beyond my control. I needed the intervention of drugs to reactivate my brain chemistry as I was clinically depressed.

I felt ashamed because I should have been able to "get over" things, but nothing came easily. You know what eventually helped me pull through? Finding and sticking with my purpose!

When I started looking outward at a plan that was bigger than myself, I was able to see the light in amongst the darkness. If you are reading this and have ever felt the darkness closing in, I am sure you can relate that when you look outward and find a worthy cause that you can support, things change.

Although it all starts with being your own best friend, I encourage you to make small meaningful differences in other peoples' lives too. Choose to smile at a random stranger. Cook a meal for an older person. Volunteer to read a story at a library. No matter what you choose to do, I promise that when you see life is about a purpose bigger than yourself, you will be able to step out of your "brain drain zone" and step up to your God given talents.

As a Kids Life Coach, I see children going through so much stress and pressure that they are too young to process. They don't have the skills to cope with our demanding world, because nobody has taught them. Sadly, many parents and teachers only refer children to me after things have gone wrong. This is so counter intuitive and it has become my sole purpose in life to create a paradigm shift where Kids Life Coaching becomes mainstream.

Why ship kids off to therapy when the going gets tough? Surely prevention is what we should be aiming for? I don't believe that we should wait until adulthood to "fix" our problems and re-engineer faulty belief systems. I believe it is about putting a foundation in place to make sure that children are equipped to deal with whatever life throws their way.

This is why I am so passionate about being the leading service provider globally when it comes to Kids Life Coaching. I am so super lucky that I get to work alongside a community of like-minded professionals who share my vision for world change that starts with our children!

My organisation The Kids Life Studio®, was born out of my own personal experiences and challenges. It was conceived because I had felt the feelings that so many children are feeling right now. Overwhelm, helplessness, hopelessness. These are all easy to overcome with a toolkit in place, which is why I think, in fact, there has never been a better time to be called "crazy"!

I want to encourage you to be mindful of the stigma associated to mental health and I ask you to please reserve judgement. In fact, if I could ask one thing of you, it would be to speak to the children that you have an influence over. When they use the words "crazy", "mad", "mental" or whatever other descriptors they have heard adults using, stop them and redefine the word.

You see, crazy doesn't have to be a bad thing. For me, it means I get to be a kid with my nieces and nephew. It means I get to play when most of the other adults have to pretend to be so serious. When they probably wish they could have more freedom like me because I happen to not have the responsibilities of being a parent. I have labelled myself as "crazy cool" and I use this to define the true meaning of who I am and not according to socially defined expectations.

The 7 Key Ingredients for Life

Taking care of a child's mental health means giving them the tools to cope with whatever life throws their way. Here are the top 7 Key Ingredients that you can share with children. The younger they are the better, but it is never too late:

Ingredient #1	Nourishing your body, heart & mind
Ingredient #2	Getting enough rest
Ingredient #3	Exercise to keep your body fit
Ingredient #4	Relaxation & down time
Ingredient #5	Being a lifelong learner
Ingredient #6	Finding a true sense of belonging
Ingredient #7	Having a mentor or role model to look up to

I feel so passionate about these ingredients and have seen first-hand in the children I have worked with how simple lifestyle changes can create mental well-being for them.

I wish you well on your adventure called life! Have fun, be "crazy cool" and celebrate all that life has to offer so that you can be an awesome role model to kids! The world needs more change makers, and I hope you walk alongside me as we make the world a better place for kids by being the solid and authentic role models that they need.

With so many resources available and so much raised awareness happening, there is a lot of support on hand to maintain mental well-being.

If you have a child and you see the benefit of coaching, why not connect with one of my Kids Life Studio® Coaches on www.kidslifestudio.com where you will also find our online lifestyle assessment and can make use of some of our free resources. If you want to educate yourself further on how to nurture your own inner Kids Life Coach, you can visit www.kidslifecoachacademy.com to do one of my online courses that will equip you with a toolkit for realistically, responsibly and ethically supporting children through life.

I want to point out that I have captured the essence of each of my coaching clients in this book with as much clarity as my memory allows. Some versions have been slightly modified to protect the integrity of my client confidentiality. In most cases I have asked respectful permission from parents and the children involved that I am still in contact with.

In closing I want to say thank you for reading my hidden truths and my versions of the hidden truths behind life, parenting and childhood with an open heart and mind. My wish is that you share the insights that most resonated with you. Children deserve authentic support that is heart centred and it all starts with you.

May you find the strength to be "The Secret Parent" role model that every child deserves.

Regards with Zeal,

Zelna (Zeal) Lauwrens
Inspired Contributor to Children Globally

ABOUT THE AUTHOR

Zelna Lauwrens is the founder and CEO of The Kids Life Studio® and The Kids Life Coach Academy. With over 100 life coaches for children around the world representing and using her methodologies, programmes and materials, she has become an expert at being an inspired contributor to the well-being of children around the globe.

Not only is she considered a world-class Kids Life Coach for the children of celebrities, entrepreneurs, corporate leaders and high profile personalities, she has also coached children who have been involved in human trafficking, living on the streets and in orphanages.

Zelna knows how to accelerate the personal achievement and fulfilment of children and parents everywhere. She is a compelling, empowering and compassionate coach who has helped tens of thousands of children fulfil their potential and achieve their dreams. Her current mission includes empowering, educating and enabling professionals around the world to harness her simple and proven techniques to get the best out of children.

Zelna's background includes a Bachelor of Education Degree with specialisation in counselling and remedial education and an Honours Degree in Psychology of Education. For the past 15 years she has been an educational consultant, a coach and a leading authority in the areas of leadership, achievement and peak performance in children. Prior to that, she was a dedicated teacher focusing on life skills in the classroom and acting as counsellor. She has also lectured student teachers at leading International Universities.

Zelna is the author of multiple motivational books aimed at children, teens and parents. She is a regular contributing writer in the media and has appeared on various news channels and TV talk shows as a panel expert on child motivation, as well as being cited in leading magazines and newspapers.

Printed in Great
Britain
by Amazon